DEDICATED TO A  WITHOUT DISAPPOINTMENT, IN WHICH EVERYONE DOES WELL.

Especially for Amber and Bas, Annette and Thijmen and, of course, Pa and Sophie.

BIS Publishers
Building Het Sieraad
Postjesweg 1
1057 DT Amsterdam
The Netherlands
T +31 (0)20 515 02 30
bis@bispublishers.com
www.bispublishers.com

ISBN 978 90 6369 413 5

Copyright © 2017 Frans de Groot
and BIS Publishers.
Designed by Studio Kluif.

THE SEVEN LAWS OF GUARANTEED GROWTH

BITSING: THE WORLD'S FIRST BUSINESS MANAGEMENT MODEL THAT GUARANTEES SUCCESS

BY FRANS DE GROOT

CONTENTS

FOREWORD

I encountered Frans de Groot for the first time at an event involving the new European Master's programme in System Dynamics (EMSD). I'll expand on this program and its relationship with the Bitsing method in a moment. But first, my first impressions. Frans's guest lecture was, in a word, overwhelming. He is a gifted speaker and the students hung on his every word, as did I. The lecture was not only very inspiring, we also received an overwhelming amount of information - knowledge built up over at least 20 years, concentrated into a period of an hour. Frankly, too much for me to immediately digest and understand. The claims that Frans made seemed almost incredible, but he had evidence to support them. And his principles were indisputably logical.

Frans related that he had been working since the early '90s on a 7-step model, which was later named the Bitsing method, which would enable organisations to successfully achieve their goals. Over the years hundreds of businesses, institutions and individuals had applied the model. They were all tracked in the process of achieving their goals. New knowledge and insights arose in the process of measuring, learning from and optimising these numerous, practical applications. Interestingly, the businesses and organi-sations that applied his method actually did, effortlessly, achieve their goals - with some showing explosive growth rates of up to 300%.

This growth percentage of 300% intrigued Frans. He wanted to know exactly why this 300% growth factor was so often achieved when applying the Bitsing method. Was it a result of the predictive function of the method itself? An exact answer eluded him. And that was why he came to us. He thought we would be able to answer the question. This turned out to be more difficult than it seemed - as we later discovered.

The question was very interesting from a System Dynamics perspective. System Dynamics enables you to imitate reality, using a computer model. Which is precisely what students from all over the world are being trained to do in our two-year European master's programme involving four European universities and focusing on management team applications. Using System Dynamics an attempt was made to copy the Bitsing model and see whether System Dynamics could add anything to the Bitsing method. In the process we also wanted to answer the '300% growth question'.

In principle, a seemingly simple task. Bitsing is, after all, a series of steps in which each of the factors that influence goal-achieve-ment are developed, bit by bit, over time. In effect, it is a stair, climbed by everyone in and around an organisation, in order to end up achieving that organisation's objectives. System Dynamics does some-thing very similar: it identifies the 'source chains' of an organisation (for example staff, finance, marketing, production, and so on) and the interrelationships that exist between these source chains. These interrelationships enable dynamic developments to take place within organisations and their environments. The similarities indicated that it should not be difficult to translate the Bitsing model into a dynamic, System Dynamics model. And that this would also allow us to further pursue the answers to questions shared by both Frans and I: "Why does the Bitsing method work so well?" - and, "Why does it regularly deliver a result that is significantly higher than the set objective, sometimes 300% higher?"

As the Bitsing method was new to everyone, the first cohort of students set about doing an one-on-one 'translation' of the Bitsing method into a System Dynamics model. This also supplied the necessary insight, for everyone involved, into how the Bitsing method works.

We gave the second cohort more direction in how System Dynamics could add value to the Bitsing method, in order to arrive at the answers we were searching for. The third cohort made our implicit knowledge of the Bitsing method's added value and operation explicit, by modelling case studies. A necessary stage in arriving at a System Dynamics model.

We were endlessly surprised by the number of insights gained from the unremitting efforts of all concerned. And by how clear and graspable they were. These insights were immediately shared with many organisations that were struggling to achieve their (growth) objectives.

This resulted in Bitsing developing into an increasingly more comprehensive method, which identified and bundled virtually all the factors that determine success. The results were truly extraordinary. In the meantime, many more organisations achieved a much-improved understanding of the principles that underlie the guaranteed achievement of their goals - and went on to apply this knowledge and, quite simply, actually achieve those goals.

We now have the answers - expressed in this significant book - as to why the method works so well (in terms of making financial, commercial and operational goals attainable) - and we know that the method can be applied to all kinds of organisations. We are also specifically pursuing the 300% growth question, as we progress with our research in the EMSD programme. Our aim is to apply dynamic analysis, using System Dynamics, to supplement the (calculation) models that currently support Bitsing.

A special mention must be made of the fact that our group of universities are also applying the Bitsing method, in order to make our Master's programme self-funding. This programme has, until now, been funded by the EU (Erasmus Mundus), which considers our self-funding application as a best practice - to be further applied, where possible, by other Erasmus Mundus programmes.

Our previous attempts to interest the market in sponsoring were rather uncoordinated. Bitsing has helped us take a far more systematic approach to gaining (increased) international awareness of our EMSD programme and getting businesses interested in sponsoring it. We are now engaged in several, serious conversations and some parties have made specific undertakings to sponsor us - simply as a result of systematically following the steps of the Bitsing model. Bitsing gives you the feeling that you're not just going through the motions, but that you're in control of what you're doing.

Prof. Dr. Jac Vennix
Professor emeritus of Research Methodology
and System Dynamics.
Former Executive Director of the Erasmus
Mundus European Master's Program
in System Dynamics (EMSD)

INTRODUCTION

My first book on the Bitsing method immediately became the number 1 best seller in the Dutch top 100 management book list. Many organisations were applying Bitsing at the time and the book spread the word. So they were quickly joined by even more businesses, institutions and other organisations. Businesses ranging from multinationals to the smallest, one-man operations were applying the method to achieve their objectives - simply and easily, in a wide variety of business sectors and in challenging markets. Bitsing appeared to work - for everyone.

The method has indeed helped many hundreds of organisations to achieve breath-taking growth in turnover and profit. In fact, it has achieved a wide range of objectives. It has also helped by maximising performance at minimal cost, increasing operating cost-efficiency without staff cuts and boosting employee performance. It assists in recruiting top talent and has effected behaviour change among stakeholders. It has even helped individuals to achieve an ideal work-life balance.

This book is my way of personally introducing you to the Bitsing method. My aim is to inspire you and make you a participant in one of the most spectacular management methods of this time. I'll explain what Bitsing is, the results it will generate and how it works. And I'll answer some important questions: What is the real basis for the successful achievement of goals? How can I be sure that I will always achieve my goals? How do I forecast results? As ambitious as it seems - the answers to these questions are all between the covers of this book, explained with the help of many examples, explanatory charts and images.

For whom?
This book is intended for everyone involved in achieving the objectives of a company, institution or other organisation. In multinationals and one-man businesses, global brands and start-ups. You could be a CEO, entrepreneur, manager, foreman, professional or student. This book is intended to inspire and coach you.

You certainly won't be reading things you already know. You've now entered previously unknown territory. Inspiring insights will keep you reading - while logical, easy-to-understand models and charts will make you want to apply these insights immediately. And you will be able to. I have tried to write in clear, easily understandable language.

Without pretention or lengthy, theoretical discourses. Because that's just not necessary with Bitsing.

You'll come to understand that we have been making everything far too complicated. That we spend a lot of time, money and energy on things that are absolutely unnecessary. As it happens - just seven, simple factors underpin the successful achievement of your goals. Just seven. The seven Bitsing principles or, as per the title of this book, 'The seven laws of guaranteed growth'. Each law is the subject of a chapter in this book.

And each chapter, with its down-to-earth examples, will convince you again of the simplicity and logic at the base of everything you read here - and proves that you need nothing more than common sense to achieve your goals. It is possible to score in a difficult market; you can grow by a factor of three - with minimal effort. You can achieve targets that you previously only dreamed of. Read on. Your disbelief will be transformed into conviction.

YOU CAN DO IT!

Welcome to the world of Bitsing.

Bitsing is the world's first and only method that guarantees achievement of your goals. I know it sounds too good to be true. And yet it is possible! It has been scientifically proven and is also demonstrated in the daily practice of numerous organisations.

Definition: Bitsing is a (scientific) business management method that enables businesses, organisations, institutions, employees and individuals to seamlessly achieve their goals, with a pre-predicted outcome

and (financial) return on the operations and investments that Bitsing - for the purpose of obtaining the goals - tells them to perform. In short: Bitsing means undeniably achieve goals, with an up-front predicted outcome and (financial) return.

This book is about achieving goals - in your business, institution or organisation - but, also in your personal life. Because Bitsing is effective in all aspects of life.

Why is it that this method so easily enables the achievement of objectives? Firstly, because Bitsing prescribes exactly what you have to do, while keeping you from making the mistakes made by others. Secondly, because Bitsing provides the answers to all the issues that can confront an organisation. Yes, all the answers. In other words it covers all the factors that determine success. But be prepared - after reading this book you'll regard most popular and established business methods and models as no longer relevant. Bitsing will influence every aspect of your entire organisation. All of its 'Bits & Pieces'. Regardless of how large or small it is. But do you know the real reason why Bitsing will enable you to succeed in achieving your goals? It's because Bitsing is the only method that enables you to predict results.

The Bitsing method proves its effectiveness every day in a wide variety of organisations. And the academic and scientific worlds have also embraced the method. Bitsing's revolutionary models have been taught at universities and colleges for many years. It is a standard part of the European university master's training programme, funded by the European Commission (see Foreword). This programme has been set up by four, leading European universities to, as they define it: 'Provide international students with the opportunity of solving real world problems and to learn how to initiate strategic change in complex organisations'. Let's start today on making the complexity of goal achievement - childishly easy.

I WISH YOU SUCCESS IN GROWING YOUR 'BITSNESS'

Frans de Groot

9

THE ROOTS

It's extraordinary that the place where the world's first multinational was founded in 1602, where the world's first share was issued and where the first stock exchange was established, is also the site of the discovery of the first method that guarantees spectacular increases in the value of any share and every organisation. The Bitsing method was discovered in Amsterdam, in the Netherlands. A country in which entrepreneurship, business acumen, common sense, openness, innovation and success are deeply ingrained in the spirit of its people. It is fitting to provide some information about the Netherlands at this point. It will explain why you'll recognise these Dutch characteristics in the Bitsing method.

The Netherlands is an important player in the global economy. It also plays a prominent global role in other respects. This is reflected in the fact that it is one of the most developed countries in the world (the fifth most competitive economy) and occupies fifth place in the Human Development Index (HDI) of the United Nations (which measures poverty, illiteracy, education and life expectancy by country).

The Netherlands has a modest population (17 million) and takes up little space on the world map. One has to acknowledge some ingenuity, therefore, in the significance of its global role. The Netherlands is the second largest agricultural exporter in the world – second only to the United States. Remarkable, for a country that has a fraction of the land area of many other countries. The Netherlands is a country that creates new land - from the sea. It gives colour to the world, as its largest exporter of flowers. And it is famous for many inventions and discoveries which make our lives easier and more enjoyable.

Some Dutch inventions: the microscope (1595), telescope (1608), submarine (1620), electrocardiogram/ECG (1903), speed trap (1958), fire hose, jenever (gin), audio cassette (1962) and Compact Disk or CD (1983). And, yes, Bluetooth (1994), DVD, Blu Ray and Wi-Fi are also all from the Netherlands. What you probably didn't expect is that the Olympic flame, four-wheel drive and Python (the programming language used by Google and Dropbox) also come from here. The Netherlands has also set up the world's largest internet hub. The largest internet exchange in the world (the Amsterdam Internet Exchange) enables all those videos, e-mails, social media posts, games and software to find their way to you.

Many TV programme formats also come from the Netherlands, such as Big Brother and The Voice.

The Netherlands is home to a strikingly large number of multinationals. Dutch multinationals are important names in the Fortune 500 and on Wall Street: Royal Dutch Shell (one of the three biggest companies in the world), AKZO Nobel, Philips, Unilever, ABN AMRO, ING Group, TomTom, Heineken, Aegon, Royal Ahold, LoyondellBasell Industries, ASML and Cargill, to mention just a few, are all Dutch. The Netherlands is also a global player when it comes to hosting the head offices of foreign multinationals. Hundreds are located here: EasyJet, Hitachi, TOMMY HILFIGER, Walt Disney, Nike, LinkedIn, The Rolling Stones, U2, Ikea, Altice, Pfizer, Abbott Healthcare Products, Sabic International, DTEK, Gunvor Group, Airbus Group, Louis Dreyfus, Trafigura and Forever 21 - to name but a few.

The country has also produced many famous names, from historical times to the present day. You probably recognise Rembrandt van Rijn, Vincent van Gogh, Anne Frank, Johan Cruyff, John de Mol, André Rieu, Robin van Persi, Dick Bruna (the creator of Miffy), Dutch model

Doutzen Kroes. And let's not forget the four Dutch DJs who are among the five best in the world: Hardwell, Armin van Buuren, Martin Garrix and Tiësto.

The Netherlands founded the first multinational in the world, in 1602 - the Dutch East-India Company (also known by its Dutch acronym, the VOC). This makes the concept of the multinational yet another Dutch invention. The VOC's international trading zeal led it to make treaties with princes, build forts and have possessions around the world.

Australia (previously New Holland) was discovered by the Dutch, who also established New York. In 1609 the native American inhabitants of the area where New York now stands were surprised by the arrival of the Dutch VOC. The captain of the Dutch ship, Henry Hudson, who was searching for a shorter route to Asia, had changed course - and named his landfall New Amsterdam, later to be renamed New York by the British.

The financial world, as we know it today, has its roots in the Netherlands. The multinational Dutch East India Company was the first company to issue freely tradeable shares. This laid the foundation for the world's first stock exchange, which opened its doors in the heart of Amsterdam in 1609. In the same year the Amsterdam Bank was set up. The world's first, modern central bank, it established the Dutch currency as the world's most stable. The Amsterdam Bank and the stock market together qualified the city of Amsterdam as the world's financial centre. And traders from all over Europe came to Amsterdam to speculate.

So many global developments have their roots in Amsterdam. And this includes the Bitsing method. Which began with the discovery of a revolutionary model...

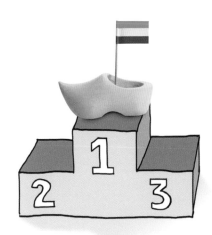

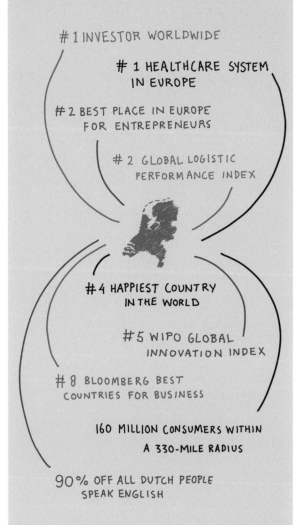

#1 INVESTOR WORLDWIDE

#1 HEALTHCARE SYSTEM IN EUROPE

#2 BEST PLACE IN EUROPE FOR ENTREPRENEURS

#2 GLOBAL LOGISTIC PERFORMANCE INDEX

#4 HAPPIEST COUNTRY IN THE WORLD

#5 WIPO GLOBAL INNOVATION INDEX

#8 BLOOMBERG BEST COUNTRIES FOR BUSINESS

160 MILLION CONSUMERS WITHIN A 330-MILE RADIUS

90% OFF ALL DUTCH PEOPLE SPEAK ENGLISH

THE DISCOVERY!

Bitsing didn't 'just happen'. It's the product of more than 20 years of scientific and practical research. For the origin of Bitsing we have to go back to the early '90s - to the start of my marketing communications agency. It was a very unusual agency. It was so successful that in its third year of existence one of the biggest global ad agencies, Lintas Worldwide, which has 160 offices in 50 countries, wanted to buy it. I had not yet realised that the Bitsing method was the basis for my agency's success.

I started my agency after a colourful career in marketing (at 3M, among other companies) followed by many years in leading, international, marketing communication agencies. This period delivered a hoard of international awards - but mainly a treasure-trove of knowledge and experience. Besides my regular work, I set up several businesses and, in doing so, experienced all the ups and downs that entrepreneurship can bring - in particular the experience of achieving success. I know what entrepreneurship is and what it means to achieve goals.

While pursuing my marketing career, I invented and marketed a unique product which, with a minimum of investment, achieved a sales volume of millions of units.

Enough to keep the Italian factory that produced it busy for 24 hours a day, seven days a week. It was quite an experience. I eventually sold the business to one of the largest home products retailers in Europe. The business had become too big - and I was kept busy and entertained by my marketing communication agency. And yes, my product invention was something I did in addition to my regular work. Have you always wanted to take that step, to initiate something? It is possible - in addition to the job or business you already have. Don't be afraid - do it - because it will succeed. The Bitsing method will ensure that. Everything I have learned and experienced over the years is built into it.

Back to the start of my marketing communications agency in the '90s: The agency had a blue chip client list: British Airways, Sony, the WWF and many more including, soon after the agency's launch, some prestigious car brands - Land Rover, MG and Mini. These brands belonged to the Rover Group - and they badly needed sales. Their sales had been declining for many years, despite all their marketing efforts. I won this fine group of car brands as clients on the basis of my unconventional approach to markets and target groups. I then wrote them a plan - based on six

steps. This was the first sign of the emergence of Bitsing as a method - without anyone realising it. This plan was implemented ...

... and then, it happened!
The group's car sales doubled. It became the fastest growing in Europe. This achievement was unique in the company's history. Yet no one really knew how this sales achievement had come about. No one knew the secret of this success. And that included me. The only clue was the 6-step plan, which was to play a ground-breaking role in the years to come. The 6-step plan came to be used as a template to develop marketing and communication plans for other clients. And it was successful time and time again, with astonishingly good results, often far better than expected.

The discovery of a revolutionary model
I discovered the secret of these successes only later. It may sound like a scene from a film, but one day I opened the document containing the highly successful Land Rover, MG and Mini plan. I was looking at the table of contents when I suddenly saw the key to its success. It was 'encoded' in the first letter of the title of each of the six chapters of the plan. And these were the initial letters of each step of the 6-step plan that I had used. Each chapter, and therefore each

of the six steps, described a phase in the marketing programme. The initials formed a word, which jumped out at me: 'BITSER'. It was instantly clear to me that this was no accident, but a model which prescribed six different BITSER activities which, when applied to a market, target group or person, delivered unprecedented results. This BITSER model is now known as the original or basic Bitsing model, because it forms the basis of the entire management method.
To understand Bitsing as a method you must first understand the original model - which, within minutes, will start convincing you of its capacity to optimise everything that you and your organisation do.

Secret of the BITSER model

The six letters of BITSER each carry in them the secret of success. You will want to know, of course, what these letters stand for and how to use the method. But first: the secret behind them. When approaching markets and target groups, you will only achieve real success when everyone does what you want them to do. Everyone! You've achieved nothing if only a very small group of people reacts to you, your organisation, its activities and messages - as you will have missed the majority of people. A question: how many of the hundred, thousand or tens of thousands of people in your most important

target group really do what you ask - react the way you want them to? For example, by buying your product or service, or changing their behaviour, or visiting your premises? It's always a limited number of people, always a small minority! All the others, the vast majority, are not affected - are missed. The reason for this is that you have only applied one, or some, of the six aspects of the BITSER model - and not all six. If so, you're not doing it wrong, you're just not doing enough.

Nobody is, thinks or acts the same!

If you require a target group to do one thing - for instance buy, in response to a sales message - you may only affect a few individuals. Certainly not everyone. Because everyone is unique and thinks and acts differently! Focusing purely on sales does not work, just doing marketing does not work, simply having the perfect product is not enough, purely providing customer services is insufficient. In fact, only focusing on any, single activity - does not work. Real success comes from the correct mix of activities. The BITSER model tells you exactly how to determine that mix. And, amazingly, there are only six activities in the mix. This is the secret of the BITSER model.

The BITSER model is a series of steps on a stair

The BITSER model is indeed simple – a stair with six steps. Every individual in a target group will climb the six steps of the BITSER stair, also those in your target markets. When they reach the top, they will have met your objectives. Everyone must climb this stair. Step by step. If they don't, your objectives will not be achieved. In which case you simply have not succeeded in helping them climb. Often because you've done the wrong thing, or too little, or - worse still - because you've done nothing to help them climb.

Everyone in your organisation – whether it's a multinational or a one-man business – is there for one reason: to help the people in your target group climb the stair and reach your objectives. Even if employees have no direct contact with the people in the market or target group, they nevertheless each play a vital role in this process.

The stair that takes you to your objectives consists of six steps, the six BITSER steps. Because people are unique and don't think and act in the same way, not everyone is on the same step of the stair. The journey begins at the bottom of the stair. These people are 'furthest' from you.

CHOOSE THE RIGHT DIRECTION

YOUR
COMPANY WILL
ARRIVE THERE

Others may already be higher on the stair, and very close to you. They will have already taken quite a few steps. This group of people need only a small push to meet your objective, for example to purchase. Everyone in your target audience is distributed across the six steps. You can place every individual in any given target group, whatever its size, on one of the six steps of the BITSER stair.

One step will contain more people than another and this will vary by market or target group. And each step will have to be approached in its own way - by the people in your organisation, via the organisation's internal and external activities. Some steps will contain too few people. So you will have to make sure that their numbers grow, in order to reach your goal. Most important is what the steps of the BITSER model will come to mean to you: that six activities are enough to get everything you need from everyone in your target group, in order to reach your goals. Just six!

Step by step up the BITSER stair
It's time to discover what the first letters of the six chapter titles of that significant Land Rover, MG and Mini plan stand for. This is where the six steps of the BITSER model and its stair first took form.

We'll start with the first chapter. This is the first step, at the bottom of the BITSER stair, where everyone starts:

B STEP 1

The first chapter of the Land Rover, Mini and MG plan started with a 'B'. It was entitled, 'Brand awareness - the foundation'. So B is for Brand awareness - where everything starts. If no one knows your name, you cannot expect to be recognised by anyone - let alone achieve your goals by, for instance, getting someone to buy your product or service. Have you ever been involved with someone without knowing their name? Unlikely. As unlikely as buying a product without knowing its brand name. Even a retailer's 'own brand' still carries the name of the retailer. How many people in every hundred are aware of your brand name? Those who don't are already lost to you. As mentioned, it all starts with the 'B'. So, fill the first step of the BITSER stair with people - by building your Brand name awareness.

I STEP 2

The second chapter of the Land Rover, Mini and MG plan started with an 'I'. The 'I' stands for Image. Your first task here is to move the people on step 1, who already know your name but not your image, to this second step. You want them to consider you, to 'want' you. Have you ever had a relationship with someone who doesn't want you? Again, it's unlikely - but it does illustrate how important being 'wanted' is. Which is also why I interpret the 'I' of the second step as 'I want you'. If people don't want you, it will be difficult to successfully complete the 'BITSER' journey and achieve your objective. So this step must be populated by people who already want you. Four more steps to go.

T STEP 3

The third chapter started with a 'T' - for 'Traffic in dealer showrooms'. 'T' is for Traffic - something that takes place towards and at the purchase point. It could be a visit to your shop, to your webshop, or a sales appointment. If they don't take this step, people are not going to do what

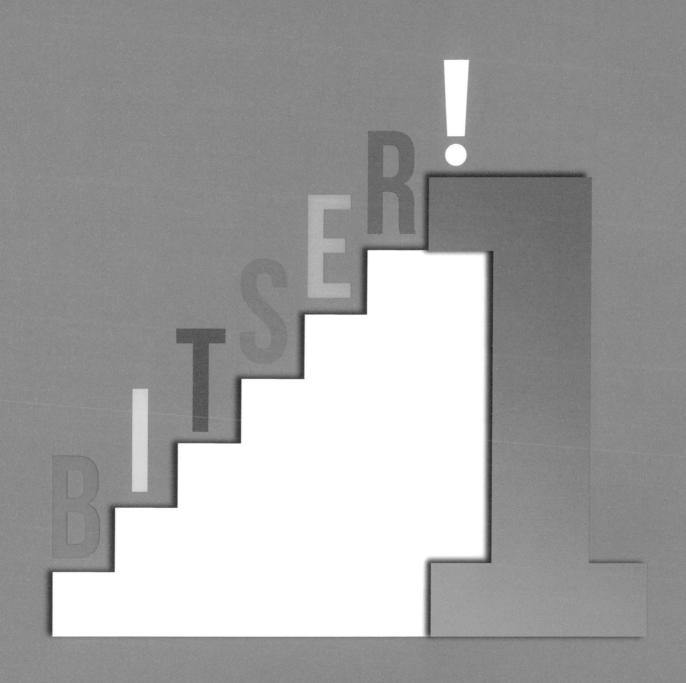

who want you to do - e.g. buy your product. No store traffic means an empty shop - in which nothing can or will be sold. And no sales appointments will produce the same, negative result. The people, who are on the previous 'I' step, the people you want, need a nudge in order to take this next step. Have you ever developed a relationship with someone - without dating them? Probably not. Which makes this step an important one to work on.

S STEP 4

'S' was the first letter of the title to chapter four of the plan: 'Sales promotion' it said. The chapter was about achieving Sales. The 'S' therefore stands for 'Sales'. This could be the sale of a product or service. But a signature on an employment contract is also a sale. Likewise when an employee performs according to your requirements, or when someone changes their behaviour - these are also sales; people doing what you wanted them to do! Do relationships not start with a kiss at some stage, when you're together, perhaps after a date? Of course they do. At some stage you 'bought' each other.

The people on the 'S' step have bought what you are selling. Stimulate everyone on the 'T' step to take this important, fourth step to the Sales level. What you've already learned is that to successfully achieve a Sale, you first have to lead your potential customer through steps B, I and T. And that calls for a range of different activities. You probably now have a better understanding of why just making a sales offer is no guarantee of success. You're missing the B, the I and the T. A sale, on its own, is just not enough. A sale, in fact, is just the beginning. The Sales step is no more than the basis for long-term, profitable success. So let's see what the first letter of the fifth chapter of the Land Rover, MG and Mini plan can tell us.

E STEP 5

The title of the fifth chapter started with an 'E', for 'Extra sales'. These Extra sales could arise from repeat purchase or the purchase of a different product or service, following the first purchase. With employees the concept of Extra sales could mean continuing to meet the goals set by you - for example continued, higher performance levels, or ongoing good conduct.

Do relationships remain at the level of the 'first kiss' (the Sale), or do they develop and is there much more interaction with each other (Extra sales)? Customers on the 'S' step, must be retained. This is done by helping them take the fifth step - by offering Extras. It costs seven times more money and effort to recruit a new customer ('S') than to get more out of an existing relationship ('E'). Reason enough to take this step with your customers. No organisation can rely on a single sale for its survival ('S', step 4). Continuity is created out of what follows that single sale ('E', step 5). While Sales generally represent the achievement of short-term objectives, such as growth, Extra sales ensure the achievement of longer-term goals (such as continuity). Target group members who have reached this step are regular users of what your organisation has to offer. They can therefore move on to the sixth and final step.

R STEP 6

The title of the sixth chapter started with an 'R' - for Referral sales. This is the final step of the BITSER model.

These are your existing clients, who are able to sell your product, service or goal to third parties, without your intervention. They are real ambassadors. Which is why they are at the top of the BITSER stair. This is your ultimate accomplishment: your existing clients are now helping you to recruit others. And it is represented by the people on this 'R' step.

Let's take another look at the chapter titles of the tried and tested Land Rover, MG and Mini plan - and how these brands doubled their turnover.

BRAND AWARENESS - THE FOUNDATION

IMAGE BUILDING ('I WANT YOU')

TRAFFIC IN DEALER SHOWROOMS

SALES PROMOTION

EXTRA SALES

REFERRAL SALES

You now understand the BITSER model - and know where it comes from.

Using the BITSER model
The six steps of the BITSER model are timeless and general in their application. They will work for everyone, in every organisation and for every objective. Every employee you have works on one or more of the six BITSER steps. Whether your organisation is recruiting or retaining customers, achieving growth, generating revenue and profit, finding staff, improving employee performance, changing behaviour or even recruiting votes for a political party. Every member of the target groups approached by your organisation will climb the six BITSER steps before your objectives are met. And your entire organisation will be involved. The better you and your employees help people in their target groups climb the six steps, the faster your goals will be achieved.

You finally have insight into what lies at the basis of successful achievement of your goals: the six BITSER steps. The letters spelling BITSER are the initial letters of the steps of the stair, which every person must climb.

From BITSER model to all-encompassing business management method
In the years following the discovery of the BITSER model many organisations have applied it. New knowledge and insights with regard to the BITSER model arose from measuring, learning from and optimising the process, from the numerous, practical case studies and from collaborating with colleges and universities in various countries. The model continued to improve and became increasingly effective. The simple BITSER model became a comprehensive method, in which virtually all the factors that determine the success of an organisation were identified and bundled. I called it: **BITSING**. The first four letters are a tribute to the discovery of the first four steps of the BITSer stair - and a reference to the fact that the method addresses all the 'bits' and pieces of an organisation, including its success factors.

The seven laws of guaranteed growth
For more than twenty years I followed hundreds of companies, organisations and individuals who had applied the BITSER model and, as a result, had achieved their goals. I examined their successes and failures and saw what worked and, especially, what did not.

I was surprised at what this exposed. Guess what? The study of these BITSER activities continued to uncover businesses and organisations that were achieving their goals - all without difficulty, some growing explosively - and some growing at precisely the magic rate of 300%!

Very significantly, seven elements emerged as common:

1 They were all guided by a continuity objective (crucial for survival).
2 They guaranteed their success by focusing on hard, financial facts (and did not diverge from this).
3 Their approach to their markets was unbeatable, they outclassed the competition.
4 They knew how to get everything they wanted from each person in their target group.
5 They only used effective programmes, both externally (with their target groups) and internally (with employees).
6 They predicted the results of their activities, before rolling them out.
7 They invested less money in their activities than they expected to earn from them (thus guaranteeing profitability).

These seven revolutionary insights amounted to the discovery of a guaranteed success formula. A formula that enables you to achieve your objectives - in seven, rapid, easy steps. I expressed these insights as seven, universal factors and called them the seven Bitsing laws. (They have also been referred to as the seven Bitsing principles.) Follow them, measure the theory and practice of your organisation - and especially of yourself and their staff - against these seven laws. And successful achievement of your goals will be assured.

Here they are again:

LAW 1 Always set a continuity objective that is crucial for the survival of the business or organisation.

LAW 2 Ensure achievement of your goal by focusing on hard, financial facts - and don't diverge from this.

LAW 3 Ensure your market approach is unbeatable; outclass the competition.

LAW 4 Get everything out of every person in every target group - in order to achieve maximum results.

LAW 5 Only deploy effective programmes, both externally and internally.

LAW 6 Predict the results of your programme activities before rolling them out.

LAW 7 Ensure profit from your programme activities by keeping your investment below your expected financial return.

I have now introduced you to the Bitsing method. In the next seven chapters I'll clearly explain the Bitsing method and its models, in theory and practice. We will deal with the method law by law - and put you in a position to use it to book unprecedented successes. You'll experience, for the first time, the real basis for the successful achievement of your goals, and how up-front prediction of results guarantees this success and a positive financial return on your investment.

LAW1

ALWAYS SET
A CONTINUITY
GOAL

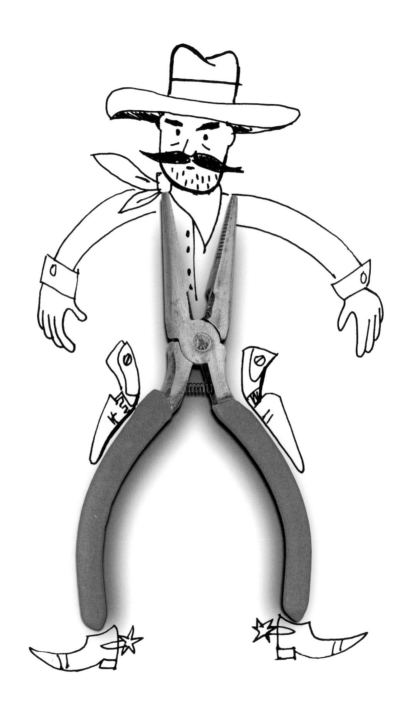

WITHOUT A GOAL
YOU ACHIEVE NOTHING

If we hadn't yet met it might be great to meet. We could decide to go for a walk. I'm sure we have much to discuss with each other. After a while you might start to wonder where we're going to and you'll ask me.

If my response was, 'No idea, I don't have a goal', we could carry on hiking for hours, but I think you'd find it increasingly less fun. Because we will never arrive anywhere. Because we have no goal.

Without a goal, you never get anywhere.

If I had invited you to go for a walk and have a drink afterwards, we would have had a good walk - and would then definitely end up at a place where we could have a drink. Because we had a goal.

You get somewhere if you have a goal.

It is essential, for everyone and every organisation, to have a goal, a target. This is necessary to avoid aimless activity that gets nowhere or, worse still, ends up at a totally unwanted destination. Not having a goal may be OK for a while, but never ends well. According to my research, more than 50% of entrepreneurs have no objectives. So how will they fare in the long run? Remember that if you start the day without an aim, you will achieve nothing in it.

The magical power of objectives

Two people both love sport and the excitement that goes with it. One of them aims to go to his favourite sports club. The other has no destination in mind. Both leave their homes to go somewhere. Who of the two has the greatest chance of ending up enjoying his favourite sport that day?

An organisation that has not formulated objectives for itself and its employees will not end up where it needs to be. There is a significant chance that it will encounter problems. Without a goal, one ends up doing the wrong things. You go through the motions, but your activities are not effective, because you don't know where you're going.

There's something magical about objectives. They enable you to work out what you have to do to achieve them. Nothing can function without an objective. But simply having a goal is not enough. If you have the wrong goal in mind, you will also not achieve what you want. In practice this means that you will be disappointed with the outcome of your activities. You can target any area of a dartboard, but if it's the wrong part, you'll lose the game. Have you ever had to deal with the disappointing results of something you had done? If so, you were probably aiming at the wrong goal. The vast majority of people working for companies and organisations work towards the wrong goals. Did you know that 93% of an organisation's employees don't know what goal their organisation should be working towards? Before I tell you about the right kind of objectives, it's important that you first know something about incorrect objectives.

Faulty objectives
An objective paves the way to doing what's necessary to achieve it. In fact, a goal gives direction to what organisations and their people have to do. If your goal is wrong, the direction your activities take will also be wrong and you will end up with disappointing results.

The route to your objectives is called strategy. Following a strategy means executing tasks. However, strategies are frequently confused with objectives. Strategies may only give direction to enable achievement of the objectives. Turn your strategy into an objective and your work will be aimless.

I frequently encounter employees who tackle their tasks with such fervour that the task becomes a goal in itself. They forget the reason for carrying out the task - executing it is all that matters. When strategies or tasks become goals the results are disappointing.

Almost every organisation is guilty of formulating incorrect objectives. This is a great pity, because bad objectives always disappoint, while a goal should always bring something positive. I don't know one person who consciously formulates an objective in order to achieve a disaster or disappointment. A goal should be positive and bring positive results. So let's stop formulating incorrect objectives, as of now.

It will help if we first look at some examples of incorrect goals and note their faults. After which I'll describe what a correct objective is.

Cost cutting is common in economically difficult times. In principle, cost cutting simply results from a shortage of money - the need to ensure profit or avoid a loss. What you often see in organisations that are cutting costs is that they invest less, while reducing costs by reducing staff. But where does this lead? How long will cost reduction go on? And what will the organisation do when it has exhausted its cost-reduction opportunities? No one can survive without flesh on their bones - and neither can organisations. Shrinking threatens the survival of an organisation. Cost saving can, therefore, never be an objective.

The second example of poor objectives is to be found in a strikingly large number of organisations. These businesses are characterised by their focus on innovation, the introduction and range extension of new and existing products and services, the development of new markets and new sales channels (e.g. online) and the acquisition of new companies. These strategies - because that is what they are - are complex and therefore high-risk. To what extent can they provide certainty about the continued existence of the organisation? There is no certainty. So these can never be your objectives.

The third example I want to mention here concerns marketing. 80% of CEOs admit to having no faith in marketers and are not impressed by their results. This is one of the most striking conclusions from international research conducted by one of the world's most authoritative 'marketing performance measurement & management' organisations - the Fournaise Marketing Group. Their Global Marketing Effectiveness Program sampled CEOs and decision makers in more than 1200 large organisations in 20 countries across North America, Europe, Asia and Australia.

I venture to say, with certainty, that the CEO's attitudes are not generated by the fact that marketers are generally bad at their craft. It is just that marketing tempts us into defining the wrong objectives. Let me explain how. In marketing, the aim is to bring a product or service into contact with a (potential) customer, in order to win a market. The term marketing is, after all, derived from the American term 'market getting'. Marketing objectives are therefore objectives about acquiring markets. Billions are invested in marketing. But what if it appears that all these marketing efforts are producing too little money - or none at all? What happens when markets are indeed won, but more money has been invest-

ed than produced? No one can give an affirmative answer to the question whether investments in marketing, and in particular in the approach to markets, can ensure the continuity of an organisation. If the practice of marketing was in itself an effective objective there would have been no economic crises in recent years. I have always been amazed at organisations that invest heavily over long periods in haphazard marketing campaigns, while they have no idea of the results this brings them. As marketing objectives do not guarantee financial return, they are unacceptable as objectives.

What about Sales objectives? We are all familiar with them. For they are among the most commonly found objectives in organisations, often formulated as 'selling a defined quantity of products or services to (potential) customers'. These, unfortunately, can also not be described as objectives. I know a company that sold twice as many products than it usually did, but achieved this with a discount of 50%. Their bottom line of course showed no financial benefit. I know of a charity that managed to recruit 35% more donors, in a shrinking market. Impressive, were it not that their expected additional income disappeared as a result of the excessive

investment in recruiting those very donors. Even though you are able to achieve spectacular growth in the sales of your products and services, this says nothing about whether you've earned enough as an organisation. Sales targets are false goals.

As a parting shot - some common objectives, which you can trash immediately: Increasing the awareness of your brands, improving the image of your organisation, getting shop or website visits - or appointments, re-styling shops, boosting sales and increasing customer loyalty – to name but a few. None of these are the objectives that you should accept as constituting your goal. Yes, I also grew up reading books by gurus who told me that these are the objectives to achieve. However, they were wrong. These objectives are extremely dangerous. Despite appearing to be a strong brand, Sony made no profit for a period of ten, consecutive years. Well-known brands, like Motorola, Polaroid, Blockbuster, Woolworth and Eastman Kodak and, yes, Lehman Brothers, have disappeared. And then there's Nokia, how much of its brand franchise survives? How 'well' are Sears and Groupon doing? They all enjoy awareness; they all chased the kind of objectives that I have described above. What went wrong? They made the wrong choices, as a result of setting the wrong objectives.

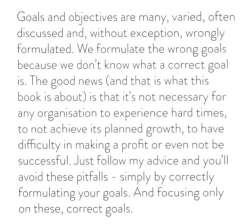

SOME OF THE MANY
EXAMPLES OF
INCORRECT GOALS

- COST SAVING
- INNOVATION
- INTRODUCING NEW PRODUCTS AND SERVICES
- ENTERING NEW MARKETS
- NEW SALES CHANNELS
- ADDITIONAL SERVICES
- ACQUIRING COMPANIES
- MARKETING
- COMMUNICATION CAMPAIGNS
- SALES OBJECTIVES
- INCREASED BRAND AWARENESS
- SHOP AND WEBSITE VISITS
- OBTAINING SALES APPOINTMENTS
- CUSTOMER LOYALTY
- RE-STYLING SHOPS
- SALES PROMOTION

Goals and objectives are many, varied, often discussed and, without exception, wrongly formulated. We formulate the wrong goals because we don't know what a correct goal is. The good news (and that is what this book is about) is that it's not necessary for any organisation to experience hard times, to not achieve its planned growth, to have difficulty in making a profit or even not be successful. Just follow my advice and you'll avoid these pitfalls - simply by correctly formulating your goals. And focusing only on these, correct goals.

What is a correct goal?

Formulating the right goal is much easier than you might think. The key to correct goal formulation lies hidden in an element common to all incorrectly formulated goals: they do not offer any guarantee of continuity of the organisation in its current form. A correctly formulated goal is thus a goal that guarantees continuity of the organisation, in its present form. 'Present form' doesn't mean an organisation that is shrinking, firing people, or reducing costs (in order to survive, as opposed to increasing its efficiency). These are survival mechanisms. No, continued existence in its current form means the uninterrupted progress of your business, organisation or institution - in its current form: continuity.

Continuity has everything to do with 'earning money'. Enough money enables continued, normal, healthy functioning. It's the only sensible option.

A correct goal is a goal that demonstrably results in the earning of money for the purpose of the continued existence of a healthy organisation.

Use this definition to test your formulated goals. If you are restructuring in order to reduce costs, but will earn less, for you are involved in the opposite of continuity: termination. Going back to some previously-described, incorrect goals: you may indeed be successful in new product and service innovation, in acquiring companies, in achieving marketing goals, in creating high brand awareness or in achieving your sales objectives - but you may earn nothing or too little in the process. Things have not ended well if the result of achieving your goals is that you have earned too little.

Continuity is an element of growth!

A goal that threatens your continuity carries the risk of financial problems - of making too little money. For instance, if goal achievement costs more than it delivers. A goal that guarantees continuity of your current situation is a financial growth objective: it involves earning more money. If you earn less than in the previous year things will be worse for you. If you earn more, they will be better, for then you will absorb rising costs and still have reserves. Organisations that want continuity need financial growth objectives. All of them - from the smallest to the biggest organisations, including not-for-profit institutions - and even governments.

I once addressed the Dutch House of Representatives on the BITSING method. Political parties took great interest in its success. I told them it concerned a single goal - earning money. Other goals were irrelevant. This didn't go down well with the politicians. A party leader tried to convince me that I was wrong by stating that politics is not about earning money. I countered by asking why he was then so interested in Bitsing. He answered that he was informed that it facilitated goal achievement and that he wanted to see if his party could attract more voters by using the Bitsing method. My next question was why he wanted more voters. He answered that his party would then become the largest and could more easily implement its political programmes. My immediate response was, 'And implementing these programmes

- doesn't that cost money?' There were a few seconds of silence, followed, in rather strangled tone, by, 'Taxpayers money?' Indeed, party-political programmes are funded by tax. Who pays for them? The voter. And who crosses the box on the ballot? The same voter. If the voter is convinced that his tax money is best invested in a particular party's programme he will vote in its favour. Just as in the supermarket, you don't have a problem spending your money on something, if you are convinced that that is what you want to spend it on. I have another example. A charitable institution's goal was to fight child abuse around the world. Earning money was considered 'not done', let alone as a goal. I asked them how they fought child abuse in practice. 'By means of projects in every continent', was the answer. My simple question as to whether these projects cost money, was answered whole-heartedly with, 'Yes of course. The money is obtained from donations'. And the donations ran into millions. 'Suppose that you didn't receive the necessary amount - what would then happen to your projects?' I asked. Here, too, there was a moment of silence before the answer, 'In that case we wouldn't be able to carry out our projects and, as a consequence, would be unable to fight child abuse'. My next question was, 'What then

is your goal?' The answer was predictable, 'To earn the amount of money necessary to run our projects'. I asked them what amount would be ideal. The answer required 20% growth. I then made this amount their Bitsing goal. Within three months they had achieved the required growth and within a year they had doubled the amount of donations to the institution. Simply by making earning money their goal.

If an organisation knows what it has to earn it can plan how to earn it. And a financial growth objective is the only, correct goal for every organisation. It is the amount to be earned within a particular period, in order to achieve healthy continuity. This may appear simple and logical, but it is indeed all-important. Everything that you and your organisation do should start with formulating how much money you need to earn. From now on I will refer to this targeted amount as 'turnover'.

It's about an amount of money
Had you, before starting to read this book, already formulated a goal, or did you have one in mind? If so, does it guarantee the continuity of your organisation? In other words, is it an amount of turnover? Do a quick round of your colleagues and employees and ask them what goal

they would set for your organisation. Their answers will include everything but not continuity-related goals. 'To be the best', 'deliver quality', 'retain clients', 'streamline distribution', 'become market leader', 'survive', 'grow' ... even descriptions like 'more turnover', 'profit' and '5% turnover growth', all mean nothing. How much money is that 5%? Make your continuity goal tangible. And do this by expressing your goal as a specific amount of money. Using an actual case from a telecom company, I'll demonstrate what happens when you don't formulate a continuity turnover goal for your organisation. The telecom company had set itself the goal of acquiring 70,000 new subscribers. The employees tasked with implementing the company's sales strategy were presented with this 'incorrect' goal. However when the company applied Bitsing and, as a consequence, formulated a continuity turnover goal - one that guaranteed its advancement - it turned out that they didn't need 70,000 but 90,000 new customers. The telecom company would not have survived with its previous, incorrect objective. Why 'turnover' as a target - and not 'profit'? It's easy to explain. Suppose the expenses of a company are 30 million euros and that it wants a profit of 2 million euros. The company will then have to achieve a

turnover of 32 million euros. If the company turns over less it will not be able to cover its expenses, thus making no profit. Profit therefore depends on achieving turnover. You need turnover to be able to make a profit - and not the other way around. So achieving turnover is fundamental to making profit. Failure to achieve 32 million euros turnover means no 2 million profit. The focus must be on turnover when setting your goal - and not on profit. We will end up with profit in this book. See the seventh law.

You work to make money

All of the foregoing in this chapter has served to bring the primary Bitsing law to the fore:

You work to make money.

To this I must add: not to spend money. Many people in an organisation are indeed far too eager to do exactly that. The achievement of your organisation's turnover goal is the sole reason that you do what you do. Everything costs money. It's unfortunate - but it's just how things are. Achieving a goal also costs money. Why would you then accept that your investments in people, marketing, production, communication, purchasing and sales don't have to generate money? Nevertheless, in most organisations

this is the accepted way of thinking. Worse still, investment is often considered a necessary evil and is not related to any form of financial return. If making money (read, 'achieving turnover') were to form the basis of all their activities, much of what organisations and their personnel do would look very different. Most employees have no idea how much money their organisation should be making. Not today, not this week, nor for the entire year. Let alone that they can help earn it. To go back to the beginning of this chapter: if you don't know what your goal is, you won't achieve it. If you don't know that Amsterdam is your destination, how would you ever get there? And if you don't know what you have to earn today, how can you earn it? The price that an organisation has to pay if its personnel don't know what has to be earned is dramatically high. The first step to a financially successful organisation is the formulation of its continuity turnover goal. We will define this for your organisation (it may also be a country, department or business unit).

Defining the continuity turnover goal
The turnover goal may be any amount, as long as it guarantees your continuity. I cannot say this often enough. A wide variety of turnover goals have been achieved by applying the Bitsing method.

These range from very low, for recently started businesses, to the many billions required by multinationals. The GNP (gross national product) of a country is also turnover and, indeed, must also be earned. Start by defining the period in which you need to earn the required turnover. This is preferably, and frequently, a twelve-month period commencing at the same time you start applying the Bitsing method. It could also be a period of two or three years, or even longer. Do not, however, choose a period shorter than twelve months. This is because we are going to split your turnover goal and allocate it to even shorter periods. The turnover continuity goal applies to the entire organisation - or the entire business unit - with all its products and services. What turnover is needed to provide continuity for this organisation or unit over a defined period? This is the amount you need to determine. We will also check its correctness. It's important. This is, after all, about your turnover continuity goal. I asked a famous toy retailer what his turnover goal was for the coming twelve months. He replied, '53 million euros'. I then asked what he had earned in the comparable, previous twelve months. The retailer again answered, '53 million euros'. I replied, 'But that is exactly the same amount. Is that right? Haven't your costs increased?

And if so, doesn't that mean that your turnover goal of 53 million euros would never cover all your expenses, and that you'll probably have to reduce your staff?' The retailer told me that he was already doing that and would be happy to again earn 53 million euros, as the market was under extreme pressure and was in fact shrinking. I disagreed. When you apply Bitsing, you achieve goals that guarantee the continuity of your organisation. We will not be dictated to by market conditions! I asked what the turnover had to be in order for the retailer's business to continue to function in its current form, with the addition of a healthy profit. The retailer answered, 'Then it should be 60 million euros'. So this became his Bitsing continuity goal. The toy retailer actually achieved a growth of more than 30% (from 53 to 69.7 million euros), while his two direct competitors had to accept a decline of about 8% of turnover. The toy retailer performed at least 39% better than them.

Now formulate the goals you need to achieve in order to continue operating. Determine three goals (which is what I always do): The target amount - which guarantees continuity (the continuity goal); a slightly higher amount - based on your desired growth (the ambition goal);

and finally - the amount that you dream of (the dream goal). On the basis of the knowledge we will share in the coming pages, you'll see that you can achieve all three of them, using the Bitsing method. It's guaranteed!

FORMULATE 3 GOALS

MY CONTINUITY GOAL

DREAM GOAL

AMBITION GOAL

HAVE YOU WRITTEN
DOWN YOUR GOALS?
LET'S PROCEED TO
LAW 2: THE GUARANTEE
THAT YOU WILL ACHIEVE
YOUR GOAL!

SURPRISE YOURSELF!

Before you start with law two, I would like you to answer a question.
You'll find it on the web page at **www.bitsing.com/growth**.
It will take you a few seconds to answer this question, but the result will motivate
you for the rest of your life. Do it before you continue with law 2.
At the end of the book you'll make use of this answer – and you'll be surprised
at what's happened to you as a result of the Bitsing method.

LAW 2

ENSURE THAT YOU ACHIEVE YOUR GOAL

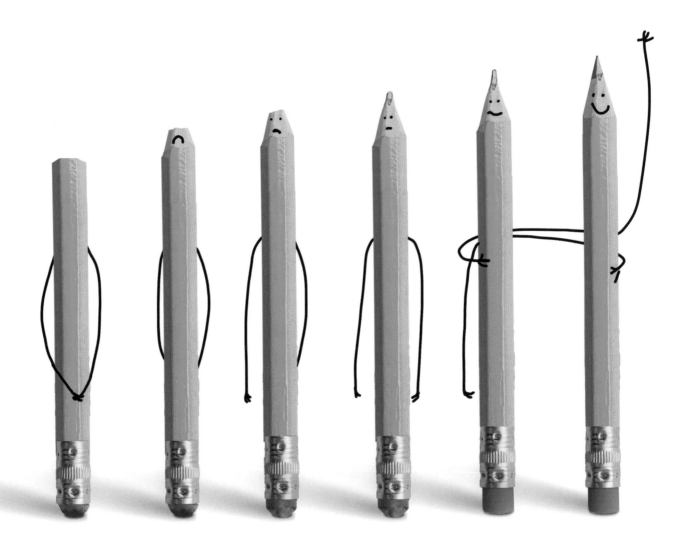

YOU WILL REACH YOUR GOAL - IF YOU MOVE IN THE RIGHT DIRECTION

With this second law of the Bitsing method I will show why you can be 100% certain that you will achieve your goals and those of your organisation – without any doubt - and that you will easily overcome any obstacles you may encounter. It is a very special law - as it will demonstrate that easily reaching your goal is a question of making the right choices. What I will share with you is how nothing can fail anymore. And, in fact, that success is guaranteed.

The models that I will present in this chapter will show that you can achieve even the most ambitious growth objectives - while expending less effort and less money. Do you want to benefit yourself and the people around you with a 25% saving of time and money? With Bitsing this is the rule, rather than an exception. And it will soon be clear how it is achieved. Start planning to reduce your working hours. It's time for the good things in life!

In the previous chapter, I made it clear that everything revolves around achieving the turnover goal, which in turn secures the continued existence of your organisation: the continuity turnover goal. A goal like this is achievable. Quite simply, even it can often be enormously ambitious. Do you, right now, have any idea what you have to do to achieve your continuity turnover goal?

I will help you make error-free decisions, easily, and indicate where your focus should lie.

Never do what you think you should do!
An excellent piece of advice. Because, as of now, you and I are going to stop thinking. We'll stop using our brains. What a delight! No more stress. Peace! Have you ever considered that thinking only consists of thoughts and that these thoughts are rooted in assumptions? Assumptions, that are very far from the reality? So if you think about what you need to do, you are just making choices based on assumptions. In fact you are gambling. The question is whether you will arrive at your goal through gambling.

COMMUNICATE!

The Bitsing method consists of a number of laws, which you should imprint on your brain, every day. They make the difference between success and failure. But the method also prompts you to act! One is that you must communicate. Without communication nothing happens and nobody will take action. So your goals will not be achieved. Without communication you will achieve nothing. Communication is a must. It is as simple as that. Nobody gets moving without communication. Stimulus always precedes action. And, if you want to achieve something, you yourself will have to take action. Doing nothing leads to nothing. You have to reach out, go out, get out of your office, your building, your shop. You have to get in touch with the people with whom and through whom you will reach your goals. That means that you can't sit at your desk all day. You must undertake action and it must be aimed at precisely the people you need in order to achieve your goals! Investment is not important in this context. Communication has nothing to do with money. But it has everything to do with whether you do nothing or something with regard to the person with whom you must communicate. And that is not dependent on money. How often have you heard people (including yourself) say that there is no budget and thus little or nothing can be accomplished? If you do nothing, you will accomplish nothing. What matters is that you communicate and act. Action! With or without money. And if you have little, or nothing, to spend – find a smart solution. But make sure you communicate.

We may sometimes enjoy a visit to a casino in the course of a night on the town - but now is not the time. For we want certainty that we will meet our continuity goal.

Gather a group of friends or colleagues around you and – if you know any - also a few consultants. Let's say ten people. Sit them down and tell them that you have a travel goal, namely the city where commerce was invented: Amsterdam, in the Netherlands. Now you need their advice.

You want to know which direction you should travel in in order to get there. Starting from where you are now. Let's say you're going to travel on a yacht or in a plane. Ask each of the ten to close their eyes and to point you in the right direction - in their opinion - to get to Amsterdam. They'll think about it - then each will point in a direction. I can predict that they will all point in different directions. Why? Because they can't see the goal, Amsterdam. Do it now - just ask the people around you. Everyone will point in a different direction. You'll see! Even if someone indicates roughly the same direction as another in the group, they will never indicate exactly the same direction.

There will always be a few centimetres discrepancy. So, you will get ten different directions, ten different opinions, each sending you off in a different direction. How likely is it that you will now end up in Amsterdam? Despite all ten directions, the chance that you may end up some-where near the Artic is greater than that of arriving at your goal, in Amsterdam. So there you are, at minus 50° C or - 58 F, at the Artic. Experiencing disappointment is greater than success. Even if one of your ten friends or colleagues had recently been to Amsterdam, the direction of the route that he or she then took and will advice will no longer be correct. The prevailing conditions at the time, such as wind and currents, would have been different - and your yacht or plane will need to set a different course. What one learns from this is that it is not simple to set a direction when the goal is not in sight. That if decisions are based on assumptions, goals will not be achieved. And, lastly, that knowledge and experience from the past, due to changing circumstances, will not drive the correct choices today. So don't act on the basis of your own thinking as a matter of course and, in particular, do not let yourself be misled by the experience of others if you want

to achieve your goal. How many of the decisions taken in your organisation stem from what someone thinks is a good idea, from what someone just 'wants'?
If you want to be successful in achieving your goals, nothing can be left to chance. You don't need input that starts with, 'I think that ...' or, 'I want to...'. It's not about thinking or wanting. What matters is that you do what is necessary to achieve your goals. If you do what is necessary, you will achieve your goals sooner - and will then have plenty of time to pursue those other wishes. And don't ever forget - assumptions will never lead to goals.

So what will?

The truth is in the facts
You have undoubtedly heard the saying, 'facts don't lie'. Facts are demonstrably correct. Assumptions not. The truth is thus based on fact. So why base your choices and decisions on assumptions? The chances of achieving your goal are much greater if you base your decisions on facts. What makes the Bitsing method so special is that you will no longer base your decisions on assumptions, but purely on facts. As a result of feeding the methods and models of Bitsing with factual information, factual answers and solutions will emerge.

These, if acted upon, will lead to factual, and thus guaranteed, results! Imagine we are in a casino, at the roulette table. We start by putting a chip on black, or red. I think we should bet on red. However, if you know in advance that the roulette ball will land on black, would you place your chip on red? We have one more chip. Suppose you know that the ball will land on number 20, would you then still put that chip on another number? With your advance knowledge, the only thing you have to do is guide your hand to put the chips on black and number 20. In practice, however, this is not always easy.

Bitsing offers inspiring solutions, but it can also sometimes ask you act counter-intuitively. What you have to do is not always what you want to do, or what you are used to doing. And regardless of how factually correct an outcome may be, It feels not always comfortable. Opinions that are based on facts may well be at odds with what one is used to. We will tend to choose red, even though we know that the ball will land on black. People tend to cling to familiar patterns. And these are not easy to break. The Bitsing method, incidentally, can quite simply change the way people think and act. I've accumulated a lot of experience in this regard.

This will become apparent in the following chapters. Which is why these chapters provide tips on how to get yourself and others, almost effortlessly, to do the right things. Following these guidelines will mean that you can look forward to a successful financial year, in which all activities will deliver positive results, revenue - and profit.

The application of the analyses contained in this book requires the use of a lot of information. Where facts are necessary, but you don't have them - no problem. There are so many correlations between the analyses that you can derive the answers needed to achieve your continuity goal - using Bitsing - without even having the required information. I've worked with companies that had very little factual information. And yet they still arrived at all the answers and achieved their goals. One of these companies even achieved three times the amount they had targeted as their goal!

FACTS DON'T LIE!

Feeding factual information into the methods and models of Bitsing gives rise to factual answers and solutions which – if acted upon – deliver real, guaranteed results!

What is factual information?

It is primarily information based on demonstrable truths and not on visions or wishes. It is simply information - as it is - not as it seems. From the perspective of the Bitsing methodology, factual information also goes a step further. The ideal information for application in the Bitsing method, is information that is current. Today's information. So not yesterday's (that's over, gone), and not tomorrow's (that's an expectation, an assumption). No, the more current the information, the more useful and valuable it is. Because it is then more factual. If current facts are not available you may refer to the past, to a very limited extent. But try to keep the information required by the Bitsing method as current as possible.

Focus, focus, focus

The information on the following pages will enable you to lay the foundations for problem-free achievement of your turn-over goal. This starts with understanding what you should focus on. To be specific, I'm going to start by forcing you to make choices. Because you can't do everything, let alone focus your attention, money and time on everything. So let us focus on what is critical for achieving success.

Having made these choices you'll have set out the beacons that determine the route to your ambitious turnover goal.

The criteria for correct choices

Choices cannot be based on mere feeling. If you navigate a boat across the ocean purely on feeling, reaching your destination will be a matter of chance. Choices (and focus) are about maximising chances. If you maximise the chances of reaching your goal you will clearly have the greatest chance of achieving it. Why waste precious time, human resource and money on something if you are not sure that it will bring you closer to your goal? The right choices are those that you are (demonstrably) sure will enable you to achieve your turnover goal. So what kind of choice is that, you may ask? These are the criteria:

The correct choice is the choice that you know will certainly maximise your turnover opportunities. Such choices will always have a financial aspect.

If you focus on what you know (as a fact) will maximise your chances of achieving your turnover goal, you will achieve it. The choices that you are going to focus on form the pillars that support your success and that of the rest of your organisation.

The ultimate tool for making correct choices

This is a significant section. It covers a tool which I invented and which has both helped many organisations to succeed and prevented major financial debacles. We're going to discuss 'the pencils philosophy'. It's the perfect tool for making the right choices, testing them and thereby preventing tragic errors. The pencil philosophy focuses you and your choices on the things that make the achievement of your goal certain. It very simply and clearly identifies your priorities and the amount of attention you must pay to each of them. It indicates how you must allocate your time and guides your financial investment. Even the correct set-up of your internal organisation becomes a piece of cake. In fact, the pencils philosophy will interrogate the strategy of your entire organisation.

The pencils philosophy

Let me explain how the pencils philosophy works. I will need your participation. Take six pencils. If you don't have any, refer to this picture.

As in the picture, the three pencils on the left are blunt. The three on the right are sharp - to varying degrees. In fact they are arranged according to degree of sharpness, with the most blunt pencil on the extreme left and the sharpest on the extreme right. I now want you to use one of the pencils to write down your continuity turnover goal on an A4 sheet of paper. Which one of the pencils would you not select for this task? Indeed - you would avoid one of the three blunt pencils, on the left. And yet they are all pencils. So why didn't you choose one of the pencils on the left? You will answer, 'Because they don't have points - they are blunt'. You have now exposed something very significant: that the choice is not about the pencil, but whether it has a point or not. Success is about the point, not the pencil. If you choose a sharp pencil, with a point, it is a fact that you will successfully put your continuity sales target on paper. You will have reached your goal. The pencil on the far right - the one with the sharpest point - will enable you to write the most. The other sharp pencils will also do, but will enable you to write less. You can try to write with the blunt pencils until the cows come home, but the end result will always disappoint.

So you will avoid choosing from the blunt pencils if you want to achieve immediate results. The pencils symbolise the choices you make. You have to make choices and take decisions to achieve your turnover goal. For example: to which product or service should I give the most attention? On which market, target group or individuals should I focus? When should I approach the market? What price should I set? Which continent, country or region should I target? And how do I set up my organisation? The multiplicity of options makes it difficult to make the right choices. But just in the case of the pencils, one option will bring you closer to achieving your turnover target than another.

Your first step is to look at the factors that directly influence achievement of your turnover goal: the turnover determinants. Most organisations that I have encountered face the following options:

1. Continent, country and region.
2. Business unit, line of business, department and type of employee (position).
3. Market segment and industry category.
4. ⟶

4 Target group, decision-maker and influencer.
5 Product category, brand, product and service.
6 Sales channel, type of distribution.
7 Pricing and customer spend.
8 Period and season.

In addition, there are a number of choices related to the effort you have to make to achieve your turnover goal. For the path to your turnover goal is indeed obstructed by a number of factors, which you need to take into account and engage:

9 Which threat or development am I confronting?
10 Which competitor am I engaging?

If you have to deal with further issues which are critical for achieving your turnover, add them to this list and apply the pencil philosophy (the application is explained below) to these too. The correctness of your choices will determine whether or not you success-fully achieve your turnover goal.

Making the right choices on the basis of the pencils philosophy

Consider all of your above-listed turnover determinants, one by one.

Each of these offer you the opportunity to make choices - from 'sharp pencil' choices to the most blunt. The choice of, and thus the focus on, sharp pencils will immediately lead to positive results. These choices will help you achieve your turnover target. Selection of blunt pencils will minimise your chances of success. What defines a 'sharp pencil choice' and what not? I'll answer this using the following example. A supermarket has six products on the shelf. Each of these products has achieved a certain turnover. This can be seen in the table below:

REALIZED TURNOVER	
PRODUCT A	€ 10,000
PRODUCT B	€ 5,000
PRODUCT C	€ 330,000
PRODUCT D	€ 100,000
PRODUCT E	€ 120,000
PRODUCT F	€ 94,000

PRIORITY	PRODUCT	REALIZED TURNOVER	SHARE
1	PRODUCT C	€ 330,000	50%
2	PRODUCT E	€ 120,000	18%
3	PRODUCT D	€ 100,000	15%
4	PRODUCT F	€ 94,000	14%
5	PRODUCT A	€ 10,000	2%
6	PRODUCT B	€ 5,000	1%

Arrange the six pencils in order of sharpness, with the most blunt pencil on the left and the sharpest pencil on the right. How should the supermarket match its products to the pencils? And does it know which product should be given the highest priority and which the lowest? How will it rank these priorities?

The product that has achieved the most turnover - product C - is given the highest priority. The product with the lowest turnover - product B - gets the lowest priority. The allocation of products to pencils and their correct order of priority is:

The products represented by sharp pencils always represent the bulk of the turnover, together usually making up more than 60%. The last three products are blunt pencils. Together these always represent products that together make up a minor part of the turnover.

Focus on hard financial facts and don't deviate from them

The choices you make must serve to maximise turnover opportunities. Turnover is a financial measure. If you want to maximize your chances of a higher turnover, you do so by testing your choices against another financial fact, namely the turnover achieved in an earlier period. On the one hand this is because you have to achieve a financial objective, and turnover is financial. On the other, it is because achieved turnover is the hardest financial fact that you have. Last, but not least, the way you achieved past turnover falls within your organisation's comfort zone. You were successful in doing so, have experienced it and are comfortable with it. It is easier to sell an existing product than one that is completely new. It is easier to start writing with a sharp pencil, than to have to sharpen a blunt one.

The hardest financial fact is the turnover you've already achieved.

For start-ups

Start-ups need to get their information from the market and from similar organisations, via the internet. In fact, you will use information from your competitors.

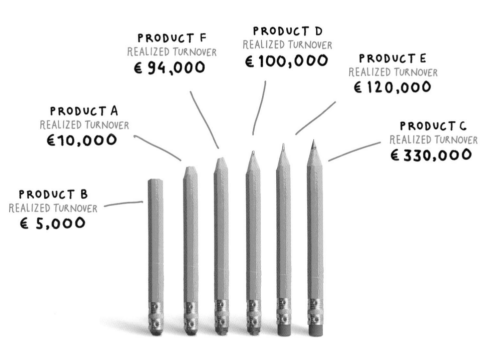

PRODUCT F
REALIZED TURNOVER
€ 94,000

PRODUCT D
REALIZED TURNOVER
€ 100,000

PRODUCT E
REALIZED TURNOVER
€ 120,000

PRODUCT A
REALIZED TURNOVER
€10,000

PRODUCT C
REALIZED TURNOVER
€ 330,000

PRODUCT B
REALIZED TURNOVER
€ 5,000

In the course of time you will acquire increasingly more data - derived from your own situation and timeframe - and this information will then drive your further progress.

A car dealer turns over 330 million euros selling cars. The car market is declining. So, in addition to cars, he now also wants to sell mopeds. The product is new to him and he plans to focus all his attention on moped sales. What are his chances of again making a 330 million euro turnover? Not big, of course. Our car dealer is, after all, not known as a seller of mopeds. He is not familiar with the business of selling mopeds, and his moped sales are so small that it will never be able to dominate his total sales on the short term. Car sales are his sharp pencil. The car dealer would be best advised to continue to focus most of his attention on selling cars. Selling mopeds is a blunt pencil. He would still have to sharpen that pencil to make it useable. The advice: pay little initial attention to moped sales; gradually pay more attention as moped turnover increase; as this happens, gradually decrease the focus on cars - until mopeds dominate the turnover. This is the car dealer's only route to financial survival. Don't 'change', just do things a little differently.

Taking the pencils philosophy a step further
The pencils philosophy allows you not only to prioritise your options and gives insight into their relative importance. It also tells you how much attention you need to pay to each of your choices, in the form of tangible percentages. This enormously simplifies the business of focusing your attention. You can evaluate your choices simply by looking at their percentage share of turnover.

PRIORITY	PRODUCT	REALIZED TURNOVER	SHARE
1	PRODUCT C	€ 330,000	50%
2	PRODUCT E	€ 120,000	18%
3	PRODUCT D	€ 100,000	15%
4	PRODUCT F	€ 94,000	14%
5	PRODUCT A	€ 10,000	2%
6	PRODUCT B	€ 5,000	1%

Let's go back to the six supermarket products. Look at the chart above. The ranking of products in terms of importance is already known to the supermarket, as a result of the session in which they were prioritised. We will now address the percentage of attention and effort that the supermarket should give to each product. The chart shows the percentage share of turnover of each product. The percentages in the right-hand column indicate the percentage of attention required per product - the required allocation of time, energy, money, departments and people per product, as well as the dominance of the product in advertising and in-store. Thus, half of the efforts of the supermarket must go into product C. How do you determine 50% of a 100,000 euro investment, a 40-hour work week and an organisation of 10 employees? The answer is: a focus of 50,000 euro, 20-hours, 5 employees on product C.

The degree of attention does not have to be identical with the percentage share of turnover. If there is a downward trend in the demand for a product, for example because it is ageing, you may give the product a little less attention than its share of turnover indicates. The supermarket could adjust the 50% focus on product C downwards, to around 45%. Products that are still growing - say, products A and B - could receive a greater percentage of attention. Say 5% more, each. This is called 'sharpening the pencils'.

Don't overdo it. For instance, don't stop giving attention to the turnover-dominating product, C, because it is ageing, while focusing all attention on the low-turnover products, A and B. This would be a mistake. Make sure that the percentage of attention given is close to each product's actual share of turnover. Then you can grow a new, currently 'blunt' product without risk and, also without risk, make a declining product progressively less dominant in terms of attention. Periodic measurement allows you to continue to adjust the focus percentages in line with the new current situation. This is safe, which at the same time guarantees success.

The role of blunt pencil choices

The organisation should prioritise and focus on sharp pencil choices. This is necessary, because it immediately leads to achievement of its turnover goals. The blunt pencils also have a role, however - and a very significant one. Blunt pencils ensure continuity. They guarantee the future turnover of your organisation. Although blunt pencil choices won't help accomplish your turnover goal right now, they will in time. They often represent new products and services (innovation) and new markets, target groups, sales channels and so on. However, don't let your organisation make the mistake of only going for the blunt pencils. This would be a big mistake.

Choices in favour of sharp pencils create instant results. Blunt pencil choices ensure continuity in the long term but not in the short term. Imagine that you have been using the sharpest pencil for some time, focusing on the choice represented by the sharpest pencil - which is product C in the supermarket example. After a while, writing will blunt the point of the sharp pencil. This symbolises that the choice it represents - in this case a product - is gradually losing its dominance. The product's share of turnover is gradually reducing over time. Ultimately, even the sharpest pencil will become so blunt and the pencil so short that it will no longer be sensible to pay attention to it. Its role will be played out. It will disappear completely. As I said before, this can be a function of ageing. Sharp pencils thus eventually become more blunt, can no longer grow, will as a result lose their dominant share of turnover and will have to be replaced by fresh, new pencils which can be sharpened. This replacement role is reserved for the blunt pencils. The choices that do not yet 'have a point'. In the supermarket example these are products F, A and B: the 'blunt products'. These pencils may not yet be getting much attention (see their percentages in the supermarket example), but by incrementally increasing attention in steps of five per cent, they will increasingly come to dominate turnover and they will thus become sharp pencils, replacing those that have become blunt. By sharpening these pencils, step by step, you will be securing turnover growth and continuity.

PRODUCT	TURNOVER	HISTORIC TURNOVER	NEW TURNOVER
PRODUCT C	€ 330,000	50%	30%
PRODUCT E	€ 120,000	18%	10%
PRODUCT D	€ 100,000	15%	8%
PRODUCT F	€ 94,000	14%	22%
PRODUCT A	€ 10,000	2%	18%
PRODUCT B	€ 5,000	1%	12%

THE SUPERMARKET

Look at the percentages under 'new share of turnover'. How would you rank the priority of these products, considering their new shares of turnover? The turnover shares and therefore also the priority and share of attention of the previously dominant products, C, E and D, became smaller - and those of the originally, not-so-important products, F, A and B, many times larger. Over time, the supermarket's allocation of attention to its products will gradually change.

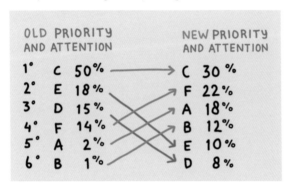

OLD PRIORITY AND ATTENTION			NEW PRIORITY AND ATTENTION	
1°	C	50% →	C	30%
2°	E	18%	F	22%
3°	D	15%	A	18%
4°	F	14%	B	12%
5°	A	2%	E	10%
6°	B	1%	D	8%

The chances that the turnover objectives will be achieved have again been maximised by setting new priorities and attention levels. Far too many organisations make the wrong choices - write with blunt pencils. These organisations run into problems. And they do not achieve their turnover goals.

Applying the pencil philosophy yourself
With the help of a number of questions and examples, I will now explain how you can apply the pencils philosophy - and, as a result, ensure that you only make correct choices: choices based on your achieved turnover. Please note: this touchstone is not a rule, it is a law!

What turnover amount must you use as factual touchstone?
You should use the amount of achieved turnover. Achieved turnover is turnover earned in the comparable period (of equal length) preceding the period in which you want to achieve your continuity turnover goal. If your turnover goal applies to this year, then the hard financial fact is the turnover achieved in the comparable, previous year. If your turnover goal is for the last six months of a year, the hard financial fact is the turnover of the last six months of the previous year. If you have a turnover goal for one month, the hard financial fact is the turnover achieved for the same month of the previous year. By 'hard financial fact' I mean the turnover you achieved in the comparable period, preceding the period in which you want to produce your new continuity turnover. Turnover is not profit. It is the total amount you have earned as an organisation, department or business unit. For the government of a country it is total tax revenue. For a charity it is donations. For a football club it includes sponsorships, ticket sales, merchandise and club cards.

For an airport it's landing fees, parking and retail turnover - and so on. Got the picture, regarding turnover? Make a note of yours here (in pencil):

ACHIEVED TURNOVER:

_____

_____

_____ ,

THE TOUCHSTONE

Has your business just started?
If you're just starting up and have no historical turnover, check whether there are organisations comparable to yours in the market. Then try to find out the amounts of their actual turnover. If this information is unobtainable, use your own continuity turnover target as a hard, financial fact.

I'll now use the pencils philosophy and some interesting cases to work with you and identify your choices and your focus. In one example, I'll use an analysis in which the pencils philosophy has been applied, with turnover per continent as the criteria. If continents are not relevant in the context of your turnover, I urge you to read this piece anyway - as it is a general explanation of the process of making choices with the pencil philosophy. Instead of 'continent' you may want to insert any dimension that is relevant to the achievement of your turnover - such as countries, regions, departments, markets, target groups, sales channels or products, etc. But first, I'll show you how easy it is to use the pencils philosophy.

For example:

PRIORITY	CONTINENT	REALIZED TURNOVER	SHARE
1	EUROPE	€ 53.500,000	34 %
2	NORTH-AMERICA	€ 47.000,000	30 %
3	ASIA	€ 31.000,000	20 %
4	SOUTH-AMERICA	€ 16.000,000	10 %
5	RUSSIA	€ 8.000,000	5 %
6	AUSTRALIA	€ 1.500,000	1 %

The pencils philosophy and the focus on continents

Suppose you measure your turnover per continent. Your 'pencil choices' will then possibly relate to more than one continent. Which continents deserves higher priority and most attention? With reference to the relative amounts of achieved turnover per continent, answer the question, 'What is the turnover by continent?"

1 List the continents.
2 Write down the amount of achieved turnover per continent.
3 Calculate each continent's percentage share of turnover.
4 Rank the continents in order of decreasing turnover.

Continent focus strategy

The continent with the highest priority (no. 1) and the highest focus percentage is the 'money continent'. It is also the continent with the highest share of turnover. And it is the continent that will produce the most money in the shortest time. It is therefore the first priority and the main focus of your organisation. Give the highest priority to the continents that together dominate turnover. In this example Europe, North America and Asia account, in total, for at least 85% of turnover. These are the sharp pencils. The remaining three continents - South America, Russia and Australia - are the blunt pencils. They must be sharpened before they can occupy a dominant role. Allocate your organisation's attention and focus to the continents in proportion to their percentage share of turnover. Round off the percentages, for convenience.

The sharp pencil, Europe, thus, gets 35% of your focus and the blunt pencil, Russia, 5%. If a particular continent is shrinking in terms of turnover, while another shows growth potential, give the shrinking continent somewhat less attention (I always recommend 5% less) and the growing continent slightly more attention (I recommend 5% more). Europe, for example, then becomes 30% (rounded down), instead of 35, and Russia becomes 10 instead of 5% of the focus. It's already been said, but is so important it's worth repeating: Make sure that the focus percentage remains close to the percentage share of the turnover. Hence my advice to give 5% more attention (than its current share of sales) to a growth strategy; and 5% less attention to a declining item. Periodically measure the latest turnover shares, and adjust your priorities and your focus strategy percentages accordingly. You have now determined your strategy as regards focus on the various continents. The strategy indicates the optimum level of attention you should pay to each continent to achieve your continuity turnover target.

The focus on other turnover determinants
Use the procedure applied to continents to determine the amounts of focus required on other turnover determinants. Follow the same steps as described for continents, as set out in the preceding pages. You will immediately see where the priorities must lie and how to allocate attention in relation to the percentage shares of turnover. The pencils philosophy thus provides fact-based insight into which countries, regions, market segments, industries, sectors, target groups, business units, departments, brands, products, seasons, etc. should dominate your turnover. A simple switch in target group and product focus achieved the highest turnover ever for shops in one of the top ten international airports. I once had a strategic session with a big American toy store chain. Which target group did their marketing plans identify? This is a question I have often asked. And most people respond directly with, 'Children'. That's right, the target description the toy stores used was also children and their marketing was indeed aimed at children. Yet this was wrong. To identify the 'focus' target groups, you

must look at who paid for the product, not who uses it. The target group is made up of the people who pay. Focusing on them leads directly to achieving the turnover goal. Who pays in toy stores? The first thought of most people is not the children, but their mothers. This is, again, incorrect. Simple research in the outlets showed that fathers paid, not mothers. More than 90% of the turnover came from the pockets of fathers! So the money target group (the sharpest pencil) is fathers. Yet they were not an element in the chain's marketing campaigns. The campaigns were then rapidly adapted to target fathers and the toy chain's turnover changed from declining to growing. To this day the chain continues to grow. What do you do in relation to those who are not 'payers'? In the toy stores these were the children and mothers. They are admittedly not the 'payers', but they do stimulate the money target group - fathers - to pay. You must therefore include them in the marketing process, but not give them a dominant share of attention. They are only influencers and play, as it were, a supporting role. The money target group has the leading role. I'll tell you more about this in law 5. Another example follows below. The danger always lurks that the things that have made an organisation great and good are quickly taken for granted. They therefore receive

less attention - and certainly not the amount of attention necessary to achieve growth and turnover goals.

A focus on sharp pencil turnover determinants (which are together responsible for more than 60% of your turnover) instantly enables achievement of your turnover goal. They ensure that your turnover, as it were, 'accelerates'. Blunt pencil turnover determinants (constituting less than forty per cent of sales) have future value. They drive innovation, strengthen your products and ensure turnover continuity. Sharp turnover determinants - 'with points' - accelerate turnover. 'Blunt' turnover determinants stimulate innovation and development.

A leader in mobile telephony derives more than half of its turnover from sales of 'loose' SIM cards, coupled with subscriptions for a fixed number of call minutes. The consumer has a choice between three such subscriptions: 100, 200 or 300 call minutes. The variant with 200 minutes accounted for the majority of the turnover. It was the product with the sharpest pencil point, the money product, and therefore should have been the focus of the telecom company. The other two subscription plans were apparently blunt pencils. To boost falling turnover it was decided to remove the money product from the range, in the expectation that customers would then buy subscriptions for 300 call minutes. The opposite happened. Consumers switched to the smallest subscription, for 100 call minutes. And turnover fell even further. On the basis of the pencils philosophy it was predicted that this would happen.

Once you start applying the pencils philosophy you will begin to appreciate that Bitsing makes things very concrete. And the more tangible something is, the easier one can pick it up.

The pencils philosophy can also help you gain insight into the factors that stand in the way of achieving your turnover target.

THE PENCILS PHYLOSOPHY APPLIES IF YOU HAVE SEVERAL BRANDS

LET'S SHARPEN SOME PENCILS!

Some organisations have several brands, representing multiple products and services.
Take Unilever, which has at least forty brands ranging from Dove to Omo and from Blue Band to Axe and Lipton.
160 million times a day someone, somewhere in the world, chooses a Unilever product – and two billion people use a Unilever product every day. How does one then determine where to focus one's attention – and how to weight that focus across the areas requiring attention?
If your organisation has many brands, products and services, apply the Bitsing pencils philosophy.

This could be a specific development in the market and the competition that disrupts your target audience from becoming and remaining a customer. And there are probably other factors. You can apply the pencils philosophy to select which obstacles you want to overcome.

Focusing on threats and opportunities
A threat is something you cannot influence, yet it presents an obstacle to achieving your turnover target. Try to find out which developments in your market(s) constitute a threat to achieving your turnover target. Examples are a decline in demand for owned homes due to banks granting fewer mortgages; new legislation which makes it more difficult to acquire customers; a recession - which limits consumer spending. Only look at the threats which will demonstrably - and therefore actually - cost you turnover. List the threats and apply the pencils philosophy, distributing the series of threats across the pencils. Now approach the dominant threat in a different way. What opportunities does this threat bring you? What can you identify that will make achieving your turnover target easier (thanks to that threat)? Each threat brings (new) opportunities to defeat that very threat. If you make use of these opportunities you will easily reach your turnover goal. You have created

the so-called 'money opportunity'.

'SHARP PENCIL CHOICHES'

Choosing sharp pencils directly ensures turnover continuity and growth. Give these choices the highest priority and the most attention, ranking them pro rata to their share of your turnover. Pay most of your attention to choosing the pencil with the sharpest point. The most blunt pencil - though still with a point - should receive the least of your attention. Give 'pencils with growth potential' 5% more focus than their turnover share. Pencils that will reduce in sharpness and importance - or must be reduced because their share of turnover is too large - form a continuity risk. So give them 5% less attention than their share of turnover. This approach will optimise the successful achievement of your goal.

'BLUNT PENCIL CHOICHES'

Choices representing 'blunt pencils' will not lead directly to achievement of your turnover objective, but will facilitate that achievement in the future. They support long-term continuity. Sharpen these pencils by gradually paying them more attention. They will eventually come to dominate your turnover. Do not expect that they will easily deliver big sales and growth purely as a result of giving them a lot of attention. Sharpening them is not easy. Never give them too much focus. Give them just enough focus to sharpen them. For example 5% more than their current share of turnover.

Your organisation's efficiency

The strategic focus criteria that emerge from the pencils philosophy also say something about organisational efficiency and therefore the future efficiency of your organisation. Say you have a department of ten people, whose activities focus on the 'business market' - a growth market. It turns out that the bulk of your turnover comes from the consumer market, not the business market - in fact eighty per cent. Despite this fact, only two people work in this consumer department. The department's staffing does not agree with the factual relationships. Eight people should work in the consumer department and two in the business department. It's easy to move the people - and no one has to be fired. While applying the pencils philosophy in a session with a financial institution, I found that 4% of its turnover came from 43% of the customers. Yet half of the employees were working on these customers (the 'blunt pencil'). The other half was therefore responsible for 96% of the turnover. This explained much, both about the excessively high internal workload and the fact that there was no substantial turnover growth. A simple reorganisation reduced workload pressure and grew turnover by 25%. If your choices deliver a disappointing result, you are paying too much attention to 'blunt pencil' options. If a choice resulted in success, it was a 'sharp pencil' choice. Ask this question in relation to all your decisions:

'Am I going to use a sharp pencil or a blunt one?' People who use the pencils philosophy find it enters their business language: 'Is that a blunt pencil or a sharp pencil? It's blunt? Don't pay too much attention to it. But if it's sharp, we will give it plenty of attention.'

The pencils philosophy and profit

In this chapter you've applied the pencils philosophy in the context of turnover. It provided the perfect focus. Now do this on the basis of profit - your margin. This will deliver a different distribution of criteria across the pencils. Superimpose the analysis of the turnover pencils over the profit analysis. You now get an even better insight, on which you should focus when it comes to growing turnover at optimum profit. You can now sharpen the strategic focus of your organisation even further.

THE BEST DECISION-MAKING-TOOL

I have an excellent tool for simplifying decision-making. Imagine that I have three gifts for you. All three are made of paper. Unfortunately, you can only choose one. I keep the other two. Which would you like? Choice one is toilet paper. Always useful. Choice two is also made of paper, but it's something you may find even more useful – namely a fresh stack of printer paper. So you have the choice between toilet paper and printer paper. Do you already know what you want, or do you first want to see the third option? OK then, option three is a roll of paper money. Which would you like? I thought so. The paper money.

You made that choice easily. Despite the fact that all three gifts were made of paper, you chose the most valuable paper, the 'money paper'. This demonstrates something very important. Things become really interesting when described as 'money': paper versus money paper. If you add the word 'money' to the subject of your decision the decision becomes very easy. An example: You must make a choice between social media and an online shop.

Whether you really have to involve your organisation in one of these alternatives becomes immediately clear if you add the word 'money' to them: 'money social media' and 'money online shop'. And then ask yourself: If social media or an online shop are to be worth something to me, do they demonstrably and actually maximise my chances of achieving my continuity turnover objective? If the answer is an undeniable 'yes', then you have a 'sharp pencil'. You then give the selected option a significant role in your activities. If the answer is no, or you don't know for sure, then either social media or the online shop, or both, belong among the 'blunt pencils'. This does not mean that they are unimportant — they remain on your agenda, but you don't focus any significant energy on them. You pay less attention to the 'blunt pencil' variety of social media or online shop and allow the option to develop more slowly. There are similar comparisons. A region, or a money region? A target group, or a money target group? The money target group significantly increases the chances that you will achieve your turnover objective. You are comparing a decision maker and a 'money decision maker'. The latter is the one that demonstrably ensures achievement of your turnover. There are also products and money products, a department and a money department, a threat and a money threat, a competitor and a money competitor. And so on. Once an option is qualified by the word money you can make a better assessment of the decision to give it more or less priority.

WICH FOCUS HELPS YOU ACHIEVE YOUR CONTINUITY OBJECTIVE?

COPY THIS PAGE AND WRITE DOWN YOUR ANSWERS TO THE FOLLOWING FOCUS CRITERIA. THIS WILL SET THE COURSE YOU SHOULD TAKE TO ACHIEVE YOUR CONTINUITY TURNOVER OBJECTIVE.

	FOCUS	ATTENTION
MONEY CONTINENT		%
MONEY COUNTRY		%
MONEY REGION		%
MONEY BUSINESS UNIT		%
MONEY DEPARTMENT		%
MONEY POSITION (JOB TYPE)		%
MONEY MARKET SEGMENT		%
MONEY INDUSTRY		%
MONEY TARGET GROUP		%
MONEY DECISION-MAKER		%
MONEY INFLUENCER		%
MONEY BRAND		%
MONEY PRODUCT CATEGORY		%
MONEY PRODUCT		%
MONEY SERVICE		%
MONEY SALES CHANNEL		%
MONEY PRICING		%
MONEY CUSTOMER SPENDING		%
MONEY PERIOD		%
MONEY SEASON		%
MONEY THREAT		%
MONEY OPPORTUNITY		%

AND DON'T FORGET TO ADD YOUR OWN SUCCESS-DEFINING CRITERIA.

CHANGE.
DON'T EVEN THINK OF IT!

'Change management' is one of today's most annoying clichés. It's as if change, in itself, will bring success. Which is far from the reality of change. The Dutch word for change is 'veranderen' – which illustrates my point rather neatly. The word can be split into 'ver' (far) and 'anderen' (others). Which expresses my advice on change: stay far away from it – and leave it to others. If you're driving in your car and get lost, do you change the car? No. At most you drive in a different direction. Which is exactly how you're going to use this second law of the Bitsing method. Not to change – but to take a different route. You're going to do things differently – but using existing resources and capabilities. Success really has nothing to do with change, but with doing things differently. A small difference in how you do things can have a large, positive impact.

Change management has a negative impact on your organisation. Attempts to change people have never met with success, but you can get people to think differently and do things differently. Which is why I prefer to speak of 'difference management'. Organisations that attribute their success to change have actually just done things differently. They haven't really changed at all. Has Coca Cola changed? Or Apple? Or Microsoft and Shell? Yet organisations that pursue change do take big risks – and often don't succeed. Brilliant businesses with world-changing products have failed because they tried to change. Compac, one of the largest global suppliers of PCs, failed – when it changed into being part of a software giant (HP). MCI Worldcome, a billion-dollar American discount telecom company, went bankrupt as a result of change in the form of a series of massive mergers. Eastern Airlines changed from a postal service into one of the four largest airlines in America, but could not survive this change and disappeared off the map. General Foods Corp. bought brands that lay outside the area of its core business, was itself purchased by cigarette company Philip Morris and, yes, went up in smoke.

Tire manufacturer Firestone tried to grow by producing a completely new kind of tire – and rolled to a halt. Consumer Electronics Manufacturer RCA was prized for its history of innovations – it was the first company to globally market electronic television sets – but began to diversify its operations beyond the area of its traditional business. The ensuing expansion was so quick and so remote from its core business that the company became impossible to manage. AltaVista, a search engine that was once bigger than Google, destroyed itself by adding unnecessary complexity to its interface. More examples? Well, just Google them.

Change can lead to dismissal of employees, unnecessary cutbacks and more misery than solutions. Is this what you want in your organisation? Just doing things differently will lead to continuity and growth, to more turnover, more profit and, above all, to pleasure, positiveness and a good (working) life. The best way to deal with change is therefore not to change. Which is in any event our automatic reaction. This is called involuntary adaptation, or evolution. Who among us still thinks and acts as they did ten years ago? We've automatically adapt to the changes in our environment. Which, for most people, is absolutely no problem. The coming of the car, television, the mobile phone and now the internet and social media caused us to involuntarily adapt our behaviour. We travelled more easily, communicated more, became better informed and more easily accessible. Most adaptation is easily absorbed by individuals and society. Although surrounded by new developments, we embrace these new opportunities and situations – and naturally adapt to them. Sometimes this takes a little time, while for some it can't happen quickly enough.

If someone tells you to change, they are actually asking you to become something other than yourself. A different person. Such imposed change is never successful. You are who you are – and change takes time. If you're currently involved in change processes within your organisation – stop! My point is that you should do what it takes to achieve your continuity goal. And this is something other than change. It's just doing things slightly differently. In order to deal seamlessly with new developments. To do things differently, for example to take a new route instead of changing the car, is something you can ask of everyone – and something that everyone can do. Imagine: you're walking outside in the sunshine, when suddenly there's a rainstorm. You put up your umbrella, so as not to get wet. The change is that your surroundings have changed – from dry to wet. Your reaction is to put up your umbrella, in order to stay dry. Have 'you' changed? Or did you just do something differently?

It's the same for your organisation. You're not currently doing things wrong – as always suggested by proponents of change management. You're just not yet doing what is necessary to achieve your continuity goal. The strength of Bitsing is that you do not have to change. You just have to do things differently. And this chapter will help you achieve that. I call it 'difference management'.

Start by looking at how you can do things differently. For example, are you currently spending a lot of time and money on things which you're not sure will turn out to be successful – while areas that produce a lot of your sales and profit are being neglected? To what extent are relatively small developments in your business, your market or the economy seen as very significant in your organisation? Online purchases of retail products and services, for example, will only account for 8.8% of the total worldwide retail market in 2018. This is less than a tenth of the market. To what extent will you focus heavily on this development?

TAKE MY ADVICE TO HEART ♥
SEE 'CHANGE MANAGEMENT' AS MANAGING TO KEEP FAR AWAY FROM CHANGE. LEAVE IT TO OTHERS.

Let's read further. Let me help you to succeed gloriously, by doing things differently – and by not changing.

LAW 3

BE UNBEATABLE

EVERYTHING THAT'S COPYABLE IS LESS APPEALING

How do you beat your competitors? Are you able to eradicate all the obstacles that you encounter on your way to achieving your turnover target? These are probably questions that no one can answer. Well, almost no one - because soon you will. Winning the fight for your market share starts by defeating everything that obstructs you. And that's a lot of obstacles. It is actually easy to overturn all of these obstacles in one simple movement. The key to achieving this, is 'being unbeatable'.

You are unbeatable, you just haven't realised it yet

Only when you are unbeatable can you rest assured that you will always emerge as the winner. That you can defeat every obstacle - even those you thought impossible to overcome. With this third law of the Bitsing method I'll take you on an amazing journey, in which you'll see how your organisation can be rendered unbeatable, within less than two hours. And without requiring any change. You are already unbeatable. You just don't yet know why.

The most expensive consultants are employed to find out what makes an organisation distinctive and unique - and to turn that into complex (re)organisation schemes, market strategy programmes and ridiculously expensive marketing campaigns. These processes take many, precious months. And what do you get as the end result? Actually nothing. Certainly not anything you could call unbeatable. We will do it differently. I will show you the foundation of 'unbeatability'. Then we'll go in search of what makes you unbeatable - and translate that into the appropriate organisational and marketing strategy. And this won't take precious months. We'll do it in a couple of hours. From now on you will be able to call yourself 'unbeatable'.

The five unbeatability factors

There are decades of scientific and practical research behind the Bitsing method. Hundreds of organisations use it, across the thousands of projects based on this method. In the process I discovered that unbeatability is supported by eight pillars. I'm going to share them with you here. And I can assure you that each, successive pillar will surprise you more. Get ready to be inspired!

THE 1ST STEP

Overcome barriers - not your problems!
Unbeatability starts with overcoming barriers, not your problems. Do you know that the only barriers to achieving your turnover goal are those that reside in your target group? There are no others. If these barriers did not exist, everyone would be doing what you want them to do, everyone would be a customer, every employee would do what you ask and your continuity turnover target would have been achieved long ago. However, this is not often the case. Yet many organisations continue to make their own problems more important than the obstacles they encounter in their markets and target groups. Most marketing campaigns communicate the organisation's problems, rather than clearing obstacles. Some examples of these messages - and their real meaning: 'Big discounts' -

we have a sales problem. 'Tell others how good we are'- we do not get enough word-of-mouth. 'We are honest' - we have been involved in some scandal. 'Take a test drive' - we have too few showroom visitors. 'The best service' - please keep hoping for it. Almost all marketing campaigns expose the advertiser's problem. Just analyse the examples around you. You will, like me, conclude that almost everyone just communicates their problems - and are therefore not busy removing the barriers that stand in their way. Yet that is exactly what they should be doing: removing barriers. And after all, who wants to hear about someone else's problems?

THE 2ND PILLAR

Always fights three barriers
Although we tend to act as if there is only a single barrier in a marketplace or audience - namely who should buy my product or service and does not do so - one unconsciously confronts another two unknown barriers. These are often much bigger obstacles - and I deliberately use the plural here. There is more than one barrier - in fact there are three. In every market and in every target group you will always confront the same three barriers:

- THOSE WHO 'DO NOT WANT'
- THOSE WHO WANT BUT 'DO NOT BUY',
- AND FINALLY THOSE WHO HAVE BOUGHT, BUT 'DO NOT STAY'.

'Do not want', 'do not buy' and 'do not stay' are the three barriers that you will encounter everywhere. In other words, someone must first want you before he buys and must buy before he stays on as a customer. So you will have to overcome all three of these barriers to successfully achieve your continuity goal. I have labelled these three barriers, for clarity in our later discussion.

You will always have to deal with:

- THE PREFERENCE BARRIER,
- THE BUYING BEHAVIOUR BARRIER,
- AND THE LOYALTY BARRIER.

The preference barrier (do not want)
Someone has to want you first, have a preference for you. If you're not on their list of preferences, you'll never be bought. Take a car brand, a fashion brand, a perfume, a supplier, or any other product or service. How many of the brands in each group are on your preference list? Not all brands. Preference does not guarantee purchase, but without preference there's certainly no purchase. Preference is the foundation - on which purchase may take place.

HOW PREFERENCES WORK!

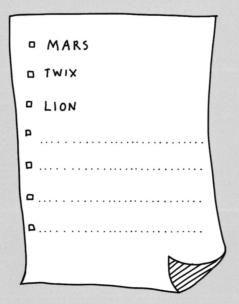

- ☐ MARS
- ☐ TWIX
- ☐ LION
- ☐ . . . .
- ☐ . . . .
- ☐ . . . .
- ☐ . . . .

To do business with someone they should first of all want you, have a preference for you.
If you are not on their list of preferred brands you will never be bought.
People often have several preferences, with a number of alternatives on their list.
They shop around. Look at your own behaviour. Take a make of car, a fashion label,
a perfume, a supplier and the like. How many brands in this group would be on your
preference list? Preference is no guarantee that you will buy, but without a preference you
certainly won't. I will first have to 'want' a certain political party before I vote for them.
Preference is necessary as the basis for purchase. Getting someone to 'buy' or 'purchase',
as these terms are used in this book, means getting them to do what you want them to do.

The purchasing behaviour barrier
(do not buy, do not do what you ask)
Although there is always a group of people that already want you, it is not often that they will immediately buy you. At the outset, there is no buying behaviour. People just won't automatically buy. To get them to do it you also have to do something. You have to stimulate buying behaviour among the people who already prefer you but do not buy. This is for example the phase in which you will recruit new customers. Buying behaviour is needed in order to lay the foundation for them to remain.

HOW PURCHASING BEHAVIOUR WORKS!

It will already be clear to you that someone who has no preference for you will certainly not buy you. Although there is always a group of people that already wants you, it seldom happens that they will therefore automatically buy you. In principle, buying behaviour never just comes about of itself. You always have to do something to make it happen. Those who have no preference for you must first develop that preference. And among those who already do prefer you, but don't buy you, you will first have to stimulate buying behaviour. This is the phase in which, for example, you recruit new customers.

The loyalty barrier (do not stay)
There is always a group of people who have already bought - and are therefore customers - but do not continue to buy. They remain one-off purchasers and will, in the course of time, become someone else's customers. This barrier applies to existing customers. They lack the loyalty to maintain the relationship.

The best strategy - the unbeatable strategy
There are always three barriers that must be crossed: The preference barrier, the purchasing behaviour barrier and the loyalty barrier. This means that the policy that your organisation should pursue should not be based on one, but on three strategies: One focused on preference, one focused on buying behaviour and one on customer loyalty. This may seem obvious, but this principle is not applied in most organisations. Instead, all departments, particularly marketing, sales and service, tend to operate as independent silos with a single focus - sales. If you conquer only one of the three barriers the effect will be proportionately small and your goals will not be achieved, or only achieved with difficulty.

Which barrier are you dealing with?
Are you and your organisation primarily busy stimulating purchasing behaviour?

Is everything you do focused on sales, sales and even more sales? If so, I will now show you what you are missing. Imagine 10 people out of 100 are already customers - so 90 are therefore not yet your customers. 60 of the latter group do not prefer you, while the other 30 do want you. So you are currently only focusing on those 30, namely those who already prefer you. Which means you are missing out on the other 70 people - your 10 existing customers plus the 60 that do not want you. This is a waste of opportunity - and not very effective. The buying behaviour barrier in this example is very small, yet the organisation had focused all of its efforts on it.

I will demonstrate that, also in your case, the buying behaviour barrier is very small and that you can easily focus a bit less on this barrier, or in other words on sales. I will illustrate this on the basis of an advertisement of a car brand which I recently saw. This car brand produced the best car in the world and, on top of that, it gave a sizable discount on the price to make it affordable for everyone. And even though this best car in the world has an unbelievably accessible low price, you're not going to buy it. Because, well, it's a Lada! And you don't want a Lada. Now replace Lada by another brand you don't want. Even though this brand offers an indisputably great competing product or service, you're not going to buy it because you don't want it! Blackberry, Sears, Monsanto, Walmart, Marmite, General Motors, Goldman Sachs; they're all among the countless number of brands that have difficulty selling because at the moment they're less wanted or not wanted at all. The Lada car brand example is very significant: If you don't want a brand, you'll never buy its product or service no matter how great it is and low priced. Wanting has nothing to do with a product, service or price range. Wanting is all about the brand. Lada is a brand. So is BMW. Philips, Heineken, Apple, Samsung, they're all brands. Have you noticed that not once have I mentioned the product those brands are selling? A product or service is not a brand.

Products and services encourage purchasing behaviour; brands stimulate preference. The 3 series BMW is a product, Heineken's beer is a product, Apple's iPhone is a product. But it's the brand that creates preference - brands make people wanting you. If your organisation is primarily communicating about its products or services, then its strategy is geared towards encouraging purchasing behaviour and it's missing out on all the people who don't want you,

that don't have any preference, because you've paid no attention to your brand.

Numerous organisations are just not aware that the lack of brandpreference is the reason people didn't buy the product or service. They think the cause lies in the offer or price. In addition to encouraging purchasing behaviour with regard to your product or service, you first need to create preference for the brand. The more people have preference for your brand, the more people will buy your product.

And last but not least, an eye-opener regarding customer loyalty. The buying behaviour strategy is often also applied to existing customers, which has a backfire effect. Will a customer become loyal if you continue to sell to him? If you have a partner at home, I doubt whether he or she stayed with you because you repeatedly wanted something from him or her. A durable relationship is more demanding than that.

If, in a single stroke, you simultaneously create preference, stimulate buying behaviour and build loyalty - with everything you do and with everyone related to your organisation - you will reap unexpected results from every target group.

LOYALTY HOW IT WORKS!

There is always a group of people who have already purchased — who are clients - but do not continue to buy. For them it's a one-off activity; or they just disappear in the course of time, to take up with someone else. This barrier applies to existing customers. They lack the loyalty to continue the relationship and to continue doing what you ask of them.

For you will also bridge all three barriers that stand in the way of achieving your turnover goal. Do you know what that means in terms of your success? It means it's assured! The trick is to know how to deal with the three barriers in a single stroke and to know the degree of engagement each requires. This is our next topic. It's called the barrier focus strategy.

THE 3TH PILLAR

Formulate the appropriate barrier focus strategy

At this point you still don't know on which of the three barriers you should place emphasis. You will certainly want to discover to what extent each of the barriers play a role in your markets and target groups. And, in turn, the relative extent to which you must focus on each of them. The answer to these questions will be as clear as daylight by the end of this section. You will discover which focus percentage you should apply to each barrier. And you'll do this with the help of the BITSER model (see the chapter headed 'The Discovery'). You will derive three percentages that indicate the amount of attention you will need to overcome each of the three barriers. This variable degree of focus on each of the barriers is called the barrier focus strategy.

The BITSER model and the barriers

You will need to use the six steps of the BITSER model* to detect the three focus percentages relative to the barriers. The letters of the six steps of the BITSER model stand for:

BRAND AWARENESS

IMAGE

TRAFFIC

SALES

EXTRA SALES

REFERRAL SALES

*If you want to review how these steps were derived and what they mean, please refer to the start of the chapter headed 'The Discovery'.

The B and I steps lead to preference. If people are aware of your Brand and you have a good Image - then they will want you. You will be preferred. The T and S steps lead to purchase behaviour. If you have Traffic - e.g. store or website visits, or appointments - and these people then move on to the Sale step, you have overcome the buying behaviour barrier. The E and R steps lead to loyalty. If a customer progresses to Extra sales, he interacts further with you - and then he enthusiastically sells you to others - which is what Referral sales means - you now have a true ambassador and you have overcome the loyalty barrier.

The barrier focus percentages

As I said, you have to pay attention to each barrier. But how much attention? This can be expressed as a percentage. If you know the percentage of attention a barrier requires, you can formulate an internal and external strategy much more easily. Should I focus 50% or 10% of my organisational resources on creating preference? The difference can be substantial! So use the steps of the BITSER model to establish the focus percentages - by creating a BITSER ranking.

How to create a BITSER ranking

You will first analyse which of the BITSER steps dominate in a particular market or audience - and which do not. By allocating a score that reflects the dominance to each of the steps, you create a so-called BITSER ranking. The first place in the rank will be given to the step that poses the biggest obstacle to the target market. The sixth position is given to the step that poses the smallest problem. Positions two, three, four and five are allocated to the remaining steps on the same basis. An example BITSER ranking (for the Dutch National Ballet) can be seen in the table on the next page. Now let's put the BITSER ranking into your practice. Take your market or target group (see law 2 which market or target group has priority). Prepare a ranking by answering the next series of questions with a number ranging from 1 to 6.

Look at all (!) the people in the market or audience, not just your customers. This concerns everyone. Be factual and honest when assigning a number score. Do not make a ranking based on what you wish the ranking to be – but based on what it is right now for the market or target group. Here we go! What is the biggest obstacle? Which one comes next? And so on. 1 Presents the biggest obstacle. And 6 the smallest.

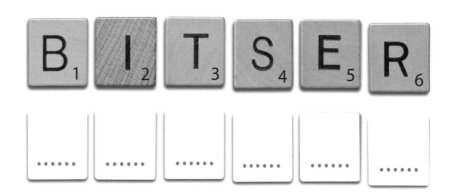

B PEOPLE HAVE NEVER- OR HARDLY EVER- HEARD OF MY BRAND NAME.

I PEOPLE HAVE HEARD OF, BUT DON'T CONSIDER MY BRAND, AREN'T INTERESTED, DON'T WANT IT.

T PEOPLE DO CONSIDER MY BRAND, BUT THEY DON'T SPRING INTO ACTION, DON'T GO TO THE SALES LOCATION, DON'T OR HARDLY VISIT MY SHOP- OR DON'T REACT TO REQUESTS FOR AN APPOINTMENT.

S PEOPLE DO SPRING INTO ACTION- THEY VISIT, MAKE AN APPOINTMENT, BUT DO NOT BUY OR HAVE NOT BOUGHT.

E PEOPLE HAVE BOUGHT ONLY ONCE- THEY BECOME CUSTOMERS, BUT THAT'S WERE IT USUALLY STOPS.

R CUSTOMERS DO NOT SUCCESFULLY SELL ME TO THEIR RELATIONSHIPS.

Converting the number scores to percentages
The scores are expressed as percentages, which represent the interrelationship of the BITSER steps. You can easily calculate these percentages. If you add up the six numbers of the BITSER ranking (total 21) and divide each number of the ranking with this total, multiplied by 100, then you get a percentage. So you arrive at the total of six percentages. I've already made this calculation for you and have rounded up the percentages. Doing so the total amounts to 105% due to the rounding. But rounded up percentages are easier to remember and to work with. Convert your ranking into percentages, allocating the highest percentage to rank 1, the next highest to rank 2, and so on.

This gives the following levels of focus, per rank.

RANK 1 = 30% FOCUS

RANK 2 = 25% FOCUS

RANK 3 = 20% FOCUS

RANK 4 = 15% FOCUS

RANK 5 = 10% FOCUS

RANK 6 = 5% FOCUS

Do you notice that 30% is the highest focus percentage and 5% is the lowest. And that the percentages per BITSER step differ by 5%. It's easy to remember.

BITSER LEVEL RANK	NATIONAL BALLET FOCUS	MY RANK	FOCUS
B	4	15%	....	........%
I	1	30%	....	........%
T	6	5%	....	........%
S	3	20%	....	........%
E	2	25%	....	........%
R	5	10%	....	........%

PREFERENCE FOCUS	B I	15% + 30% = 45%
BUYING BEHAVIOUR FOCUS	T S	5% + 20% = 25%
LOYALTY FOCUS	E R	25% + 10% = 35%

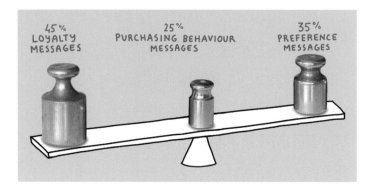

45% LOYALTY MESSAGES   25% PURCHASING BEHAVIOUR MESSAGES   35% PREFERENCE MESSAGES

Steps B and I together form the preference barrier.
Add up the percentages of B and I and you get the focus percentage for creating preference: 15% + 30% = 45%.

Steps T and S constitute the buying behaviour barrier.
Add up the percentages of T and S for the degree of focus you need to place on stimulating purchasing behaviour: 5% + 20% = 25%.

Steps E and R form the loyalty barrier-
Finally, add up the percentages of E and R and you get the level of attention you should spend on building loyalty: 25% + 10% = 35%.

The respective percentages indicate the relative dominance of each of the barriers in the target group - and the relative extent to which you must focus on preference, buying behaviour and loyalty policies. Put the percentages on each of the barriers. What do you see?

You now know how to formulate the basis of your barrier focus strategy. This gives you a clear picture of: The barriers that constitute the obstacles to reaching your continuity turnover target; how the barriers relate to each other; and which need most attention. This in turn allows you to establish a focus strategy for every continent, country, region, market, sector and target group.

THE 4TH PILLAR

The setting up of three forms of policy
How do you set up a policy to achieve preference, purchasing behaviour and loyalty in your markets and target groups? The answer to this question is as simple as putting that answer into practice. You do it by focusing your organisation according to the emphases prescribed by the barrier focus strategy. And these emphases will always be categorised under:

1 PREFERENCE POLICY
2 BUYING BEHAVIOUR POLICY
3 LOYALTY POLICY

The National Ballet (see the table on the previous page) has dedicated 45% of its efforts to establishing preference, 25% to stimulating purchasing behaviour and 35% to getting loyal customers. In doing so they filled the National Theatre to full capacity, without giving any discounts. Imagine if the National Ballet had only paid attention to activities that influence buying behaviour and hardly attended to preference and loyalty. They would then only have been able to tackle 25% of the target group issues and would have missed all opportunities associated with the remaining 75%. And they would not have filled the National

Theatre. This also shows why so many organisations have so many difficulties - and sometimes do not survive them. They miss out on significant opportunities due to incorrectly focused barrier strategy.

The three forms of policy are inextricably linked to one another. They drive each other, like a set of gears. If the preference cog does not turn, there is no impact on buying behaviour - nor, as a result, on loyalty.

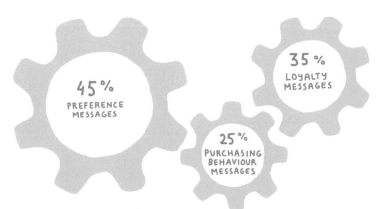

None of these three types of policy are alike. They even show huge differences. It is essential to know what these differences are, in order to limit the risk of taking the wrong action - which would lead to disappointing results.

Without a subject, there's nothing to discuss
Let's start with the subject matter of the policy. Which subject will you and your employees focus on?

No preference means there's something wrong with the brand
A policy that creates preference revolves around your brand. That isn't your product or service. Mercedes, Google and Apple are brands.

Am I discussing a product here? No, the product is the thing you buy. Product is relevant later - in the context of the policy to achieve buying behaviour. When planning preference policy, do so in the proportion indicated by the percentage required by the preference barrier in that group. The Dutch National Ballet devoted 45% of its policy – i.e. the percentage applying to its preference barrier – to its brand: The National Ballet.

If buying behaviour is lacking, there's a problem with the product or service Purchasing behaviour policy is about the product or service.
The Mercedes product is, for example, an E-class car, at Philips it's an electric toothbrush, for an airline it's a flight and at Apple it's an iPad. Don't make the mistake of thinking that a product is a brand, even though the product has a name. People don't develop preference for a product, but rather for the brand that umbrellas that product. Without the brand, BMW, nobody would have bought a 3 series car. This applies to any market. To set up the policy for achieving buying behaviour we again have to apply the focus percentage of the relevant barrier. The National Ballet focused 25% of its policy on its product, a ballet performance. The products or services that dominate in this policy, and in particular in the marketing of buying behaviour, are 'very sharp pencil' products (see law 2 for explanation), with the money product (the sharpest pencil) as leader.

No loyalty means there's a problem with the internal organisation
The policy that builds loyalty concerns your internal organisation - and mainly your 'other' products and services you have to offer. After all, a customer stays with you for what happens after buying your product or service. In this your internal organisation plays the major role. If you work alone, then everything you do after selling your product or service amounts to activities of the internal organisation. If you have outlets and external partners, then they are also part of the loyalty policy. You do so much more than just selling that one particular (sharp pencil) product or service. What about all those other paid and unpaid products and services that you deliver? One often doesn't consider the 'extras' that are already available for and provided to customers. All these extras are a product of your internal organisation and make customers loyal. They therefore form the subject matter of your loyalty policy. This is how the National Ballet, with its focus on ballet performances, built their loyalty strategy. They offered extras such as ballet workshops, 'a look behind the scenes' and a friends club. They achieved this within the focus percentage required to overcome the loyalty barrier, namely 35%.

WHAT YOU HAVE TO KNOW ABOUT BARRIERS

If preference is lacking there is a problem with your brand.

If buying behaviour is lacking there is a problem with your product or service.

If loyalty is lacking there is a problem with your (internal) organisation.

THE 5TH PILLAR

Focus on a different competitor

Your competitor is not who you think it is. The fifth pillar of your invincibility is to be found by looking at your competitive environment differently - and as a result acting differently. I'll explain: For a start, the money in a customer's wallet can only be spent once - and preferably on you rather than someone else. But who is that other? We have learned that you must be especially aware of your competitors. But who is your competitor? And who are the competitors of a car brand, an airline, a clothing store? Your answer is bound to be wrong - regardless of who you identified. And this, unfortunately, will also apply to identifying your own competitor. Let me explain - and demonstrate how, by making a small adjustment to your 'competitive thinking', you can much more easily achieve your continuity target and tap into hugh additional turnover potential. This is potential turnover, ready for the picking, the existence of which you were previously unaware.

An animal park regarded other animal parks and zoos as its competitors. It therefore executed a comprehensive analysis of these competing parks, looking at their visitor numbers, the way in which they approached their target groups, visitor expenditure and many other aspects. All interesting - but useless - topics. I knew in advance that their thick report could be immediately binned. I asked staff at the struggling animal park few questions - and came to a surprisingly unexpected conclusion. This gave them a new perspective on competitive thinking.

How would you answer the following questions?

'Let's take a hundred people from your money target group', I said (see law 2). 'How many of them buy tickets to your park? The response of the staff was: 'One.' 'We're then left with ninety-nine,' I said. 'How many of the ninety-nine remaining people buy a ticket to the other animal parks and zoos, your competition?' 'Well, four,' said the employees. 'Then I am left with ninety-five,' I said. 'These are the 100 people, minus the one who bought your ticket, and minus the four who bought tickets to the competition.' I made my a first conclusion: 'The ninety-five remaining people will spend their money doing something other than visiting your or a competitive animal park. Why do you even bother about your competitors, as only a negligible number of four people out of one-hundred choose them?' I continued:

'What is the average amount that a customer spends while with you?' '86 euros,' was the answer. My second conclusion was: 'Ninety-five out of every hundred people in your target group, who do not buy a ticket from you or from the competition, will spend their 86 euros on something other than going to an animal park or zoo.' So what was this 'something else'? The answer was: 'Buying toys', which was later confirmed by further research. I drew my final conclusion: 'Then toys are your major competitor, and not any other animal park or zoo'. An unexpected revelation. In one stroke the financial pool from which the animal park could derive its turnover had become many times larger - being the money spent on animal parks and zoos, plus the expenditure on toys. The animal park immediately took this extra competition into account in planning its policy. The policy was translated into market strategy programmes in which it now also competed with toys. Free toys were given to ticket purchasers. The result was very satisfying: 'One person out of the remaining 95 chose to spend its money on the zoo I was coaching at that time, rather than on toys. Their revenue doubled, because now two people instead of one out of the hundred spent their money on them'

QUANTIFIED EXAMPLE OF A MODEL TO TRACE THE MONEY COMPETITOR

100 PERSONS IN THE MONEY TARGET GROUP

|||| |||| |||| |||| |||| |||| |||| |||| |||| ||||
|||| |||| |||| |||| |||| |||| |||| |||| |||| ||||

1 BECOMES A CUSTOMER

|||| |||| |||| |||| |||| |||| |||| |||| ||||
|||| |||| |||| |||| |||| |||| |||| |||| |||| ||||

4 GO TO THE PHYSICAL COMPETITOR

95 DO SOMETHING ELSE WITH THEIR MONEY; THEY SPEND IT ON THE FINANCIAL ALTERNATIVE - THE MONEY COMPETITOR

That's how logically it works. To easily achieve turnover growth, don't only focus on the physical competitor. Take special care to include the financial alternative, the financial competitor - or, what we have also termed, the money competitor.

Reaching your continuity turnover target is already getting easier. Shall we adjust your target upwards?

The competitors and the three barriers
Fighting the money competitor will be the main way of obtaining preference. The competitor who obstructs preference is the money competitor. Of course, you can't ignore the physical competitor. This is the competitor who obstructs buying behaviour. It usually becomes apparent when a target group member decides to purchase a product or service that you also offer. The physical competitor here is the alternative product or service purchase - for those people who want to buy. You therefore deal with these competitors in your buying behaviour strategy. There is also a third competitor which prevents loyalty among your existing customers. Contrary to your expectations, you rarely find them outside the walls of your organisation. Yes - this competitor is internal. There is always an internal reason for a customer to leave you. Even when customers politely explain that

they are leaving for an external reason, the real reason will be internal to your organisation. You have not met a substantial customer satisfaction requirement, resulting in your customer looking for it elsewhere. This internal competitor is often something to do with how the business is organised and can be difficult to change. Hence the fact that loyalty policy must, in addition to addressing such internal factors, also tackle the internal competitor in other ways.

THE 6TH PILLAR

The right content for the right policy
Your policy content is derived in two ways: What do your brand, product and organisation mean to your target group(s) - and what do you have to offer them, what is your proposition? 'Meaning' and 'proposition' are the key ideas for the content of each of the three policies described.

What your brand means
The meaning of your brand is related to the function of your brand in society. If a brand, ABC, does not state that it is a transport company, how will I know what it does? The function of the brand here is to briefly describe to what it owes its existence, its essence, what it stands for in society.

But you may not mention the product. The ABC transport company should not communicate that it provides truck transport. Why should you not include your product or service when communicating the function of your brand? Because the brand is not your product and products do not create preference - and may also change in the course of time. The products with which a brand once started are no longer the products with which it is successful today. A brand's function is subject matter for its preference policy. What is the function of your brand?

The meaning of your product or service
Products and services validate the brand function. You buy a product because it satisfies a need. Otherwise, a product is worthless. The meaning of the product can be found in the promise that it fulfils. A vacuum cleaner sucks up dust, a car takes you from A to B. These are not selling messages, nor reasons to buy, nor competitive advantages. The promise of the product is the content of the buying behaviour policy. What does your product or service promise?

What your organisation expresses
A brand is about its role and function in society; a product is about what it does for you - its promise; while an organisation expresses the added value that it delivers. Especially in the longer term. What will the organisation mean to the customer in the future? After purchasing the product or service? It is this added value that provides the content of strategic programmes aimed at creating loyalty.

THE 7TH PILLAR

The correct market proposition
The proposition is the offer you make to your target group member. Without an offer it is difficult to create brand preference, product buying behaviour and organisational loyalty. You have to give people a reason to choose you, to buy you and to stay with you. The brand offer provides the reason for it to be preferred, the product or service offer creates buying behaviour, the organisation's offer is there to build loyalty. The offer is called the 'proposition'. It has a primary position in marketing, sales and after sales programmes. However, it's not easy to work out what to put forward as a proposition. What makes your brand special, why does it enjoy preference over other brands? What makes your product or service so extraordinary in formulation that it is chosen above other products and services? And is there something that prevents customers from leaving?

Does the proposition not literally distract one from the problem at hand; don't advertise your problem. If sales are lagging, don't immediately reach for discounts as the solution. If your brand is not yet on the list of preferred brands, don't just go and claim that it's great. As I have sometimes said, 'Take care that your propositions are not crushed by their own content'.

How do you find the most essential and unusual proposition?

Not by thinking it up on your own. Doing so means you run the risk of giving rein to your own preferences; that you could select the wrong proposition or forget a relevant one. The best way to identify propositions is to exclude personal preferences and interests as much as possible. Which means using 'the Bitsing method's score card analysis'.

Scorecard analysis

The scorecard analysis assesses your entire organisation on the factors that determine success in the market. It is an analysis of market success factors, not the factors that you or others feel are important. Imagine I have asked you the following: 'Tell me, if I were to start an organisation like yours tomorrow – become your competitor – what should I try to excel in?'

(I especially emphasise 'try to', because I'm not just interested in the factors that you are good at, but also those at which you are not good, but which do affect success in your market.) If you were then to think about your answer for twenty minutes, alone or with others who have knowledge of your market and organisation, you would end up with a list of about sixty factors. Sixty criteria that jointly determine the success of an organisation such as yours - and, indeed, that of all others in your market. I have done scorecard analyses with dozens of companies and institutions, and almost all produced the magic number of 60 success-determining factors. Organisations large or small, commercial or non-profit, government or another type of institution – are all concerned with about sixty success factors. I often call these 'market pillars', because they support both the market and the organisations in it.

The scorecard analysis consists of ten stages. I'll briefly introduce these stages of the scorecard process, confident that you'll then be both inspired by the analysis as well as equipped to use it.

STAGE 1 MARKET PILLAR ANALYSIS

The first phase of scorecard analysis is to list the factors that influence the success of an organisation such as yours, in your market - the market success factors, or market pillars. Write down all the factors that you know contribute to success. Include those factors which you may find obvious, and therefore perhaps not worth noting. Do this as if you were creating the list for someone totally new to these facts. This list provides you with a complete view of everything that's important.

STAGE 2 SCORE YOURSELF

Rate your whole organisation – everything in it and everything that goes out of it – by scoring it against all the market pillars. This indicates whether you perform well or not, on each of the market pillars. Score according to the facts - the way things actually are. Not how the market sees you. The score range is 0 to 10. A score of 10 means 'excellent', cannot be better. 0 means 'extremely bad' or 'not applicable'. If your organisation scores high on all pillars it is the ultimate organisation. How does it compare, however, to the competitors in your market?

STAGE 3 SCORING THE COMPETITIVE ENVIRONMENT

The third phase of scorecard analysis is to score the money competitor and the physical and internal competition. It will not be easy to assess a money competitor which has no further parallels with your area of business, but rate it anyway! For example, if a certain success factor is completely irrelevant to the money competitor, it will be rated 0 (not applicable). For the physical competitor use, as a benchmark, the competitive party that typifies all competitors and also dominates the market.

STAGE 4 SPOT THE DIFFERENCES

The fourth stage of scorecard analysis is to expose the differences between the scores of your organisation and those of your competitors. This will tell you exactly which market pillars have potential. And, of course, which don't!

STAGE 5 CATEGORISE THE MARKET PILLARS

The fifth stage is to categorise the market pillars according to three characteristics: Emotional, rational and relational.

The emotional market pillars affect feelings. They are not measurable and cannot be underpinned by rational arguments. Emotional market pillars are about the brand and lay the foundation for preference. Things like trustworthiness and passion.

They drive people to make a choice, which they can't rationalise. A proposition driven by an emotional market pillar creates preference.

The rational market pillars are measurable, or can be explained using verifiable arguments. They are about the product or service and they ensure the required buying behaviour. They deal with price, for instance, which is measurable; or product, which has specifications. They appeal to the mind and enable one to take, and indeed justify, a decision using rational arguments. A buying behaviour proposition is always formed by a rational market pillar.

The relational market pillars form the foundation of loyalty to an organisation. They establish a connection between two or more aspects. If preference is about 'feeling', buying behaviour about 'mind', then loyalty is about 'the heart' - it's something anchored there. It's related to delivering on promises, for example, and to trust. A loyalty proposition is formed by a relational market pillar.

Judge market pillars as emotional, rational or relational from the standpoint of your own sector. An aircraft maintenance company, for instance, regarded the market

pillar 'history' as emotional. While one would think that history is rational - at least measurable - it was indeed emotional in their context.

STAGE 6 SELECT THE PROPOSITIONS

The sixth phase of scorecard analysis is to determine the relevant propositions by analysing the emotional, rational and relational market pillar scores. Using the scorecard analysis, select the preference propositions from the emotional market pillars, buying behaviour propositions from the rational market pillars and loyalty propositions from the relational market pillars.

The market pillars on which your organisation scored at least two points higher than the three competitors are to be applied as the proposition in your market development programmes. Why the gap of at least two points - and not one? The two-point gap confirms your superiority. The greater the gap, the better you are. The pillars on which you score lower than the competition, again with a gap of at least two points, are the ones that require improvement. They will be the subjects of your internal improvement programmes.

OBSTACLES CAN ONLY BE OVERCOME BY THE MESSAGE

Indeed, only the message is able to bridge barriers. It's not the way you transmit that message, nor the medium you use. It strikes me that many organisations make the way they communicate more important than the message itself. Too many companies still focus on creativity. But creativity is just a way of transmitting the contents of a message. While, the contents of the message remain its most important aspect. Too much creativity results in campaigns that will be remembered for their creativity, but not for their content – nor for the results they achieved. The task of creativity is to clarify the message. The medium selected to convey the message is also made out to be more important than the message itself. But the medium is only able to transmit a message, not to overcome a barrier. The task of the medium – or means – is to deliver the message to the target group. The choice of medium should therefore merely ensure that you penetrate that target group. Never forget that the real success factor lies hidden in the message. All of an organisation's forms of expression are aimed at transmitting a message. However, that message is seldom expressed.

The emotional pillars underpin your brand and you use them as the proposition in the marketing programmes that create brand preference. Apply the same process to the rational pillars. The high-scoring pillars with a minimum gap of two points are the propositions that build the product or service and positively influence buying behaviour. The relational pillars scoring two points or higher than the competition build the organisation and form the propositions for the programmes that build loyalty, assuring you of an extremely loyal customer base.

Don't literally translate propositions into messages
Propositions are not literally the messages that you're going to communicate.
I may say, "I'm funny". But do you find me funny because I'm telling you this? No. For that I'll need a joke, or a bridge. This bridge is the translation of the proposition into a powerful message, one which outplays the competition. A proposition is the conclusion which people in a target group will attach to a message. And if the target group members themselves extract the essence of that message, its credibility is assured.

Regardless of its appeal, if a message is not one that your target group wants to hear, it won't be very effective. A message becomes relevant when it is connected to the target group's decision criteria. We are by now familiar with the fact that the criteria for choosing a brand are emotional, that the decision to purchase a product is rational and that remaining with an organisation is a relational decision. Three different types of decision criteria - which, if connected to your messages, will ensure that they are heard.

How to hurt the competition most
If you want to make turnover, you have to go into battle against your rivals. Your target group member can, after all, only spend his money once. The battle is about where he spends it. Scorecard analysis can help you select a few propositions with which you can create a powerful competitive statement. Just look at the market pillars on which the competition scored considerably lower than you - where the score gap is large. These pillars should be fully exploited - and to your considerable advantage. Give them priority, because they will hurt your competitors the most.

No, not yet!
And then there are the propositions that you may not yet apply. These are the propositions where your score was unsatisfactorily low. Or where the competition did significantly better than you - where the gap is large. Put them on the reserves bench for now. Work at improving them, but don't use them. Even if they are propositions that you know the market is keen to receive.

THE 8TH PILLAR

Be uncopyable
This section actually deserves a separate chapter. It's that extraordinary. However, it is also a component of being 'unbeatable' - which is the crux of this chapter. So, get ready for one of the most inspiring legs of your journey through the Bitsing method! One in which we go in search of your 'uncopyability': The one thing that makes you and your entire organisation unbeatable and invincible; which makes your propositions true and credible; the weapon with which you will defeat all and sundry. With this you will overcome each and every obstacle in your path and win, win and win again.

The uncopyability factor
The 'uncopyability' factor stands for something amazing, too good to be true - but something that is true nevertheless. It's about you. It is exceptionally valuable. And only you have it - no one else. You are going to find it, own it and cherish it. And when you have found it, your view of the world will change immediately. You will find that your uncopyability factor is the source of inspiration for everyone you're in contact with, now and in future - whether colleagues, suppliers or customers.

Everyone talks about being unique
You have to be unique and distinctive to be attractive and successful - according to the books. Well, they are wrong. Their assumption is incorrect. Do you know why? Everything that is unique and distinctive is copyable, in the long term. And copyability makes you unattractive. If the competition does what you do, why would customers continue to choose you? Today you may be 'the greatest'. In a year from now someone else may be that. You're 'the cheapest' today, but tomorrow someone else may be. You're 'the best'? Ah well, in a few months your competitor will be. 'The fastest'? No, that was yesterday. Look around you. How copyable is the element that people use to distinguish themselves from others?

Despite all the claims, everything is copyable. What is your claim right now?

I cannot emphasise it enough. What's copyable will not make you attractive nor help you overcome any barriers. Being copyable will not make it any easier to achieve your turnover target. Here is a picture of two parrots. They look the same and probably make the same sounds. If I were to ask you to choose one - which would you choose?

Time's up! You have compared them to each other. And if you are comparing - you are in doubt. This is because the parrots are so similar. They are in effect copies of each other - copyable. So what will be the decisive factor? The following picture contains the answer. I guarantee you that you will choose the parrot on the right.

Price has therefore prevailed. The choice becomes simpler when you know that the one on the right is cheaper. If organisations say the same thing and do what can also be claimed by another, they are copyable and therefore comparable. What we learn from this is that if you say and do the same things as another, price becomes decisive.

Uncopyability in everything you say and do is therefore what it's about. Those who use price as their weapon and spend lots of money out-shouting others can conclude that they are not very different from their competition, they are copyable.

Actually, I get on very well with parrots. (They are at least good listeners.) So I have helped the parrot on the left – who just lost out to the one on the right - to find its 'uncopyability factor'.

I have also taught him that he should communicate this. After all, if you don't communicate, nothing happens. The result of my uncopyability session with the parrot on the left looks like this:
(see picture on the right)
The psychological effect will immediately be apparent. The parrot on the left lays golden eggs. He has been doing this for years, but was unaware that it was anything special. Laying golden eggs turns out to be something that the other parrot cannot and will never be able to do - let alone communicate. It's uncopyable. Now that you know that the one on the left lays golden eggs you will react very differently to their pricing.

While 15 euros was previously too expensive, it suddenly doesn't look like a lot of money. If you communicate your organisation's 'golden egg', your uncopyability factor, to your target group your price will no longer be an impediment. And even though the competition may still be spending a lot of money on making themselves visible, they will not succeed. You have the 'golden egg'. It makes you uncopyable. It's your uncopyability factor.

Your golden egg is the decisive factor in capturing a market

You don't have to be a multinational to own a golden egg. Everyone has one, they just don't know it. I have helped many companies and organisations to discover their golden egg - and all of them found it. Something no one else can copy. Everyone has a golden egg. The problem is they don't communicate it. Together we will discover your golden egg. We will search for the thing that will demonstrate your uncopyability. And when you use it you will 'own' your market, to the exclusion of all others. Regardless of how good the competitors are, regardless of their excellent promotions and offers, the strength of their brands, the formulation of their products and services - and despite their bigger budgets. You will be unbeatable, thanks to your golden egg.

We are all unique, but only one of us is 'uncopyable' - and that's you!

To find the 'golden egg' we will be exploring what I call the 'uncopyable factor' in your organisation. This is the only, relevant part of your organisation that cannot be copied. To find this uncopyable factor we have to continue the scorecard analysis, which you commenced after reading the previous pages.

Which means that a lot of preparation has already been done. Where many take months, if not years, to find something that differentiates them, the analysis required to uncover your own uncopyable factor will take you less than half an hour. And so we move on to the seventh stage of the scorecard analysis.

STAGE 7 SELECTING PROPOSITIONS WITH THE POTENTIAL TO BE UNCOPYABLE

We will return, for a moment, to the scores per market pillar, as described above. Using the scorecard (see the sixth phase in the scorecard analysis) you selected those market pillars on which you scored two or more points higher than the financial, physical or internal competitors. These are now your propositions. The idea behind selecting those scoring two points or higher is that this gap indicates that there's something special about those propositions. They could easily contain your uncopyable factor. A difference of two points or more means that you have identified something significant. When making the selection, choose the market pillars with a difference of two points or more in relation to the financial competitor and the physical and internal competitors. If you emerge with too few, say less than six, fill out your selection

with the market pillars with the biggest gap (two points or more) in relation to the money competitor and the physical competitor. In such case the internal competitor is not taken into account. If you then still emerge with too few, supplement these with the market pillars that show the biggest gap in relation only to the money competitor. The physical competitor is not further involved. When this selection process is complete we can proceed to stage eight.

STAGE 8 BROAD UNCOPYABILITY SELECTION

In more than three quarters of the cases that I come across, there are usually eighteen market pillars on which two points or more are scored (as the outcome of phase seven). Arrange your selection in groups of three to four market pillars. You will do a first uncopyable selection run by ranking each group of pillars from 'hardest to copy' to 'easiest to copy'. The most difficult will be ranked number one, the easiest will be number three (or four in a group of four pillars). The result of this 'uncopyability selection' is that you have selected the most difficult-to-copy, top ranking market pillars. These form the basis for a more specific, uncopyable selection.

STAGE 9 SPECIFIC UNCOPYABILITY SELECTION

Following on what you did in phase eight, selecting the 'most difficult-to-copy' market pillars, you now again have to rank these: also from 'hardest to copy - to 'easiest to copy'. You will find that two to three market pillars will top your uncopyable selection. The selection result for the global aircraft maintenance company, which I mentioned earlier, was that they were left with two market pillars:

NO. 1 HISTORY EMOTIONAL
NO. 2 TRACK RECORD RATIONAL

One emotional and one rational market pillar remained. It will be the same for you. Which of the remaining market pillars is now uncopyable? As you will see, selection is not without difficulty. This is always the case. And reason for it, which I am happy to have discovered, is interesting. Selecting the last two latest market pillars is not difficult. Using the scorecard analysis it's not too difficult to whittle down approximately sixty market pillars to last two difficult-to-copy pillars. The issue now is which of the two is uncopyable. And the difficulty, I know, is that the remaining market pillars are always an emotional and rational one, as we saw with the aircraft maintenance company. People who go for immediate results in the short term – rather today than tomorrow – almost always choose the rational variant as being the uncopyable market pillar. The one with the 'track record', as in the situation of the aircraft maintenance company. Usually these are employees in the organisation directly involved in sales – for instance, the sales teams. The rational variant is in fact very clear. You can work with it straight away. The track record of the maintenance company simply shows that the business has a good track record. It cannot be clearer. It is different with the emotional market pillar; it's about feeling and not easy to rationalise with supporting arguments. The history of the maintenance company? What do you mean by history? What is that . . and which history? It is not clear and therefore not immediately applicable - and so one cannot immediately score with it. However, it is often possible to build up an emotional market pillar using multiple rational pillars. Knowledge comes from history and experience comes through history. In any event, the choice for the emotional pillar as the uncopyable variant often lies with people with a vision of the future, strategists and decision-makers. Whether the emotional or rational pillar should be selected as the number one, uncopyable pillar is easy to determine - with the knowledge that the rational pillar is always the result of the emotional pillar. Without the emotional market pillar the rational pillar could never exist. The rational 'track record' of the aircraft maintenance company is the result of its emotional 'history'. History is thus the uncopyable market pillar. The uncopyable market pillar is always the emotional one!

STAGE 10 FIND THE 'GOLDEN EGG'

The tenth and final stage of the score card-analysis is the description of the factual evidence of uncopyability, your 'golden egg'. This will prove why the emotional market pillar is the number one uncopyable pillar. The concept of 'history' is not sufficient, as shown by the aircraft maintenance company example; there is much more to it. The evidence behind it describes the 'uncopyable factor': your 'golden egg'. The 'golden egg' – the one relevant characteristic that makes you uncopyable – is the evidence behind the number one, emotional market pillar. Don't use insubstantial arguments as to why this market pillar is uncopyable: be factual, tangible, clear. Say it as it is. It's how you define the true, uncopyable factor. It seems hard, but it's not. Record as many arguments as you can think of. The number of arguments has a function.

You will see a thread, evidence of a recurring fact that will form the basis for description of your uncopyable factor. In the example of the global aircraft maintenance company, the brainstorming was done to prove why their 'history' was uncopyable. And together with them I could see a common thread running through the numerous arguments constructed to deliver the evidence of that. One word kept on emerging as a common theme: 'building'. You will recognise a similar recurring element in your own selection process. I asked the people in the maintenance company, 'Keep the idea of 'building' in mind - now tell me: why is your history uncopyable?' The answer was immediate: 'We are the only aircraft maintenance company in the world that has built aircraft.' And someone added: 'We've actually been building aircraft for at least a hundred years.' And so the aircraft maintenance company found their 'golden egg':

The only aircraft maintenance company in the world that has built aircraft.

'So your competitors didn't construct aircraft?" I asked. 'No', was the reply, 'They can, at most, perhaps fly one.' 'So your greatest competitors, who stole contracts right under your nose, have never built aircraft - and yet they maintain airplanes?' Well, then I know who I want doing my aircraft maintenance; the people who have built them.

The old, copyable slogan of the aircraft maintenance company was 'knows how'. Now you know where that 'know-how' comes from. The golden egg was immediately translated into an uncopyable market positioning:

'What we put into your aircraft is more than know-how. It's the heritage of one hundred years of building aircraft. We are built on solid ground.'

At the start of the scorecard analysis I asked the maintenance company which market pillar would be uncopyable. A few were mentioned, but not 'history'. Of the sixty factors that collectively determine the success of a company such as theirs, only one pillar remained - which immediately led to discovering their 'golden egg'. How special is that? This will also happen to you.

Being 'unbeatable'
The 'golden egg' makes you uncopyable. Of course, this will be the central theme in all your communication. But above all it will render your propositions credible.

The 'golden egg' – your uncopyable factor – is the ultimate proof that your proposition is true: This aircraft maintenance company has an uncopyable track record, as a result of a heritage of one hundred years of aircraft construction.

The most important thing you've now come to know is what policies you need to generate the indispensable brand preference, product or service purchasing behaviour and loyalty that you want from your markets and target groups. You also know how to deploy them relative to each other. You know which propositions you will use in battle, to eradicate and overcome all three barriers in your target market. And, most importantly, you have discovered your 'golden egg', with which you will leave your competitors behind. Using these propositions and your golden egg, you will develop marketing programmes which will delight you with their positive results. I'm now going to tell you how to use this to get the utmost from every person in your target groups.

LAW 4

MAKE THE MOST OF EVERY PERSON IN YOUR TARGET GROUP

TREAT PEOPLE UNEQUALLY, BECAUSE NO ONE IS, THINKS OR BEHAVES THE SAME

You know what your continuity turnover target is (law 1) and what choices you have make to make sure that you reach your goal (law 2). You also know which brand, product and organisational strategy you will apply; which propositions will impact your target group; and what your 'golden egg' is. As a result you're unbeatable and can uninterruptedly pursue and achieve your turnover goal (law 3). Now you will have to convert all of this into action. For unless we take action, nothing will happen.

The subject matter of this chapter is the preparatory work for all activities of your organisation. We will clarify what you have to do to convince all the people you need in order to achieve your goal of continuity.

In my teenage years I was a shy boy. I drew cartoons but, although I was good at that, it didn't do my verbal communication a lot of good. Until I went to university. In the last year of my course we had to do a lot of group projects. The preparatory work for these projects was not so difficult. A little research, some analysis and conclusions and you were done. It was easy. However, I felt very uncomfortable presenting the results of my project to the large audience of my fellow students. The fear of speaking to this mass of people without any control over how they would behave made me very uncomfortable. I therefore prepared my presentation very thoroughly. I memorised it entirely so that I could focus my attention fully on the people in the audience and not on the content of the presentation. While I gave my presentation, I could look the audience in the eye. I could then respond immediately if I noticed any strange reactions. I could adjust the tone of my presentation, often even its content and the way I was delivering it. Presenting became like acting. I managed to capture the attention of the group, and finish my presentation successfully. This became my standard approach. I memorised every presentation and again fell back on acting. I got better at it. I got so good, in fact, that my acting changed to interacting. Regardless of the audience, my presentation was no longer aimed at the group, but at each individual person in the audience. It was as if I was delivering various presentations, all wrapped up inside one big presentation. The people in the audience felt personally addressed, which kept them on the edge of their seats when I was presenting. A possibly boring subject would even become less boring, when it was aimed at the individual. My presentations became didactic - educational stories and complete theatre pieces. People enjoyed my presentations. That shy little teenage boy became a good presenter. I learned that with an audience, one has to focus on the individual and not on the complete audience, despite its presence.

Forget the masses

You need people in order to achieve your turnover objective. They all belong to target groups. A target group member will not necessarily do what you ask. For example, a person may not necessarily become your client. You've probably already experienced this: you make a fantastic offer - but only a few people responded. This has to do with the assumption that everyone in a target group will be interested in the same offer - i.e. that everyone is the same. If only that were true.

Unfortunately, we are not all interested in the same things. And we certainly aren't the same. Indeed, only a tiny minority is receptive to what you have to say. All the rest are just not interested. Don't expect everyone in your target group to stand and cheer when you make your approach. What matters is that you sensitise each individual to your message. In fact, an individual approach is the only effective way. Every person is different, has his/her own thoughts and opinions - and will therefore also need to be approached in a unique way.

There are so many!

If your target group consists of a million people, trying to approach them in a million different ways is, of course, tricky. Even with twenty it's going to be complex. But you don't have to. We have the BITSER model. Which has a very unusual characteristic. It has been shown that every person climbs six steps of a stair before they reach your goal and if you want to reach every person in a target group individually and thus help them ascend the six steps, you only have to do six things. Irrespective of how large your target audience is. To clarify this I will take you once more through the BITSER model and let you experience the logic behind the fact that you should always approach

a target group with six activities, and that your organisation should be concerned with just six activities. For a more detailed description of the model I refer you to the chapter entitled 'the discovery'.

The BITSER model

The BITSER model has six steps. I call them the steps of the BITSER stair. Everybody eventually takes these steps in order to reach your ultimate goal - your turnover continuity goal. Everything you do should be focussed on these six steps. Almost every organisation unconsciously focuses on just one step when approaching their target groups - and often on the wrong one. Which gives a poor result. Logical - when you see that just one, small group has been helped one step further, while all others do nothing. The steps were named in accordance with the barriers that people encounter while taking them. They're grouped here, together with the profiles of the people that are linked to each step of the BITSER stair. When you know what kind of personality you are dealing with, it is easier to work with them and to obtain a successful result more quickly.

At the bottom of the stair

Here's where you find the Suspects. The first profile. They are not yet on the first step of the BITSER stair. The Suspect is the type of person who falls within the target group description, but is unfamiliar with the name of your brand and organisation.

B STEP 1

B is for 'Brand awareness'. Without being known you cannot expect to be recognised, nor can you expect that your goals will be achieved. These are people who have already heard about your brand, but be aware (!) - they haven't yet considered it. They are the Potentials.

I STEP 2

The I stands for 'image', or better yet - for 'I want you'. Someone must first want you before they will buy and that's where the image comes in, remember? So, on this step are the people who already prefer your brand, but they are not ready for action. They are called Preferrers.

T STEP 3

T stands for 'Traffic'. A visit to the sales location, or an appointment. Without this, people are not going to do what they need to do, for example buy. The fourth BITSER profile is to be found on this step – Movers. They went to the sales location, but they still didn't buy your product or service. Would they have spent their money on competing products? Whatever the case, they were not sufficiently convinced to make a purchase.

S STEP 4

The S stands for 'Sale'. It can be a transaction, but it could also be the signing of an employment contract, a staff member's performance or a change in behaviour. Buyers are found on this fourth step of the BITSER stair. They are the fifth profile. They belong to the group of people who have bought the product or service once, but did not follow up with further, desired behaviour.

E STEP 5

E is for 'Extra sales'. These could be repeat orders, or the purchase of multiple products and services. Continuing to perform according to your formulated goals and expectations is also covered by the term 'extra sales'. Which is why the sixth profile is termed Users. Those are the people whose interaction with your organisation goes further than that one, first purchase. Users make more frequent use of your products and services. Ensure that people always make extensive use of what your organisation has to offer, so you can move them on to the sixth and ultimate step.

R STEP 6

The R stands for 'Referral sales'. These are existing customers who successfully sell your product or service without your intervention. At the most you have to ask them to do it. They are Sellers, the seventh profile. Your true ambassadors. Sellers are your most valuable target group and are thus at the top of the stair. If every customer were a Seller it would not be necessary for you to put effort into influencing preference, buying behaviour or loyalty.

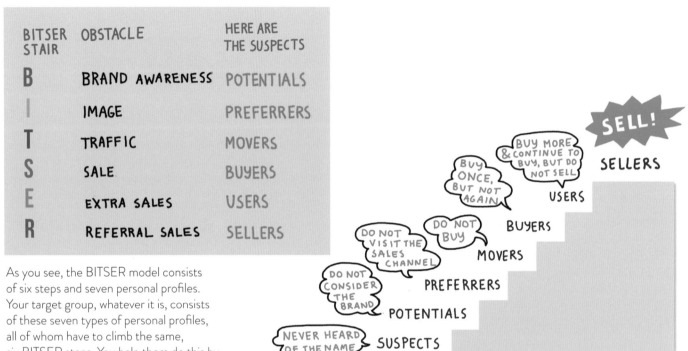

BITSER STAIR	OBSTACLE	HERE ARE THE SUSPECTS
B	BRAND AWARENESS	POTENTIALS
I	IMAGE	PREFERRERS
T	TRAFFIC	MOVERS
S	SALE	BUYERS
E	EXTRA SALES	USERS
R	REFERRAL SALES	SELLERS

As you see, the BITSER model consists of six steps and seven personal profiles. Your target group, whatever it is, consists of these seven types of personal profiles, all of whom have to climb the same, six BITSER steps. You help them do this by directing six activities at your target group.

Core elements of other target groups

In the above section I outlined the personal profiles belonging to the BITSER stair. These will be relevant in your commercial approach to target groups - for instance when recruiting new customers and retaining existing ones. The profiles for the target groups in any other discipline are the same, but what you want to achieve with them is slightly different.

What you ask of someone you want to recruit as a customer is different from what you ask of someone you want to recruit as a new member of staff. You want the former to purchase a product; the latter to sign an employment contract. What you expect from someone regarding their driving behaviour is different from someone whom you are asking to vote for you in an election: safe car driving versus voting for your party.

Below is a short description of the core elements of common BITSER model personal profiles for:
1 personnel recruitment
2 increasing internal motivation and staff performance
3 behavioural change
4 voting
5 a politician - not because I'm into politics, but to illustrate the scope

of the BITSER model regarding profiles. Because, regardless of the complexity of the target group that you're dealing with, the six BITSER steps and seven personal profiles are the same every-where and are thus applicable to a broad spectrum.

AT THE BOTTOM OF THE BITSER STAIR THE SUSPECTS
1 Never heard of the employer's name
2 Don't know what the organisation stands for
3 Haven't heard of the name of the institution
4 Haven't heard of the name of the political party
5 Haven't heard of the name of the politician

ON STEP B THE POTENTIALS
1 Know the employers' name, but not considering the employer
2 Understand what the organisation stands for, but don't have a good feeling about it
3 Know the name of the institution, but not considering it
4 Have heard of the political party, but not considering voting for it
5 Have heard of the politician, but not considering voting for him/her

ON STEP I THE PREFERRERS
1 Considering the employer; does not attend the job interview
2 Feeling good about the organisation, but does not work
3 Considering the institution but does not act, does not try
4 Considering the party but doesn't go to the voting location
5 Considering the person but doesn't go to the voting location to vote for him/her

ON STEP T THE MOVERS
1 Applied, but no signature on the employment contract
2 Works, but does not perform
3 Trying to change but is unsuccessful
4 Goes to the voting station but does not vote for the party
5 Goes to the voting station but has not vote for the person

THE STEP S THE BUYERS
1 Employment contract signed, but does not perform
2 Performs, but not more than necessary
3 Has changed, but not consistently
4 Has voted for the political party, but will not do so again
5 Has voted for the politician, but will not do so again

ON STEP E THE USERS
1 Performs but does not recruit new employees
2 Performs, better than expected, but does not motivate colleagues to perform
3 Consistent change in his/her behaviour, but does not encourage others to do the same
4 Always votes for the political party, but does not recruit new voters
5 Continues to vote for the politician, but does not recruit new votes

ON THE STEP R THE SELLERS
1 Successfully recruits new staff
2 Gets colleagues to perform
3 Encourages others to successfully change their behaviour
4 Successfully recruits new voters for the political party
5 Successfully recruits new voters for the politician

I used the BITSER model and its personal profiles in a project for an international company which, according to international norms, values and regulations, could under no circumstances supply to terrorist states. A compliance programme was developed, in which thousands of employees were individually addressed to comply with the 'norms, values and regulations'. And it succeeded! The BITSER stair personal profiles are applicable, regardless of the target group and in any situation. And so too are the six activities to help them climb the steps of the stair. It is about these that I will tell you next.

Help everyone to climb the steps of the BITSER stair

For this only six things are necessary. No more. I call them activities. You will be busy with six activities, no more and no less. Just think of the efficiency! Conduct them in the best possible way and you will achieve results that others can only dream about - with less effort, less time and less money.

Six activities which will attract everyone you need

Each of the six BITSER activities ensure that the people on the steps of the BITSER stair progress to another step. If you conduct the six activities consistently - and don't limit yourself to doing it only once – each and every person in your target group will walk your BITSER stair, step by step, and you will grow. It simply cannot go wrong. Imagine that you succeed, growing not by a few percentage points, not by ten or thirty per cent, but like

many other organisations that have embraced the Bitsing method, by up to three hundred per cent. And then you do it again, and again. The question isn't whether you'll grow, but whether you can deal with that much growth.

Be proactive

Depending on a person's condition, climbing a stair can require some effort - and can be quite tiring. Each step is a threshold. That is why you need to see each of the six steps of the BITSER stair as a difficult-to-overcome obstacle. People need assistance. The steps won't be taken without a fight. And certainly in the commercial world nobody will ascend your stair voluntarily. If you make it easy for the people in your target group to take the steps you'll reach your goals faster. You do this with a BITSER activity plan. The plan contains an activity relating to each of the six BITSER steps. The B activity aims at being known to your target group, the I activity is to get people in that target group to want you, the T activity is to drive visits to the sales location - or appointments, the S activity stimulates buying, the E activity is about remaining a customer (and carrying on buying) and the R activity is there to get customers to successfully sell to their connections.

Determining which activities you need is the work of a moment. I have already done the preparation work for you - over the period of more than twenty years in which a wide variety of organisations have deployed the BITSER model. What remains is just to tell you how you can identify these activities using the BITSER model - so that your organisation can implement them. And that starts with ...

A bit of awareness

It is impossible for someone who is still at the bottom of the BITSER stair to reach the top in a single, large step. It just doesn't work. You need to help every person in your target audience to move upwards, step by step, one step at a time. For which you'll have to do the necessary work. And it is at this juncture that things in organisations go wrong. They often only do one thing - and also, often, the wrong one. How sensible is it to target someone with an activity relative to the step he has already taken? Offering someone a product that he has already bought is not very effective and certainly not efficient. There is huge wastage in organisations when it comes to the investments made in approaching target groups.

A BITSER activity plan - in three steps
It is not complicated to draft a thorough BITSER activity plan. These are the required steps:

1 You choose the target audience.
2 You divide the target group members across the steps of the BITSER stair.
3 You then translate the results into a BITSER activity plan, with identified priorities.

Choice of target group
Start with your money audience. The issue is focus, focus and more focus (see law 2). The other target audiences will come later. I have very often seen companies achieve their yearly turnover goals within ten months, by focusing on the right target audience and implementing a proper BITSER activity plan. In such cases my advice is, 'You now have two months to indulge in your hobby projects - to do what the Bitsing method says you should not do.'

Dividing the target group across the BITSER stair
People rarely do something on their own initiative. They often need an external stimulus - action by or communication from your organisation - or an instruction from their boss.

Taking initiative is not for everyone. Nothing wrong with that, but it is vital that you realise it. So you can do something about it. You will need to do something for the people in your target market, to move them forward. This is especially true when you want something from them. If you ensure that each person on the six BITSER steps receives the right incentive, you will attain the maximum result. To do this properly, it is important that you know which steps contain the majority of the people in your target group and which steps contain fewer people. In other words, you need to know which step presents the bigger obstacle in the target group - as compared to the other steps. If you know this you can also respond to it, taking the correct action. You can then set priorities and focus on the steps that need it most. The instrument to use in this instance is an analysis tool, based on BITSER ranking.

An analysis using BITSER ranking
It doesn't matter who or where they are, each person's journey follows the six steps of the BITSER stair. The way in which the people in a target group are distributed across the steps differs. A particular target group may contain many more people on the first rung than may be found in another target group - and the same applies to every

other step of the stair. Why is understanding this so critical? Suppose there is no one on the third step of the BITSER stair - how many can then proceed to step four? Zero! And this is the crux of the matter. If too few or no people are to be found on any of the steps, there will be few or none who can climb to the next steps. As a result you won't achieve your goal, no matter what you do - or even sacrifice (your margin for instance). On the other hand, if there are enough people on the steps, then you will reach your goal. We will look at the numbers on this under law 6, in whichI shared the secret to predicting your results in advance.

You need to do a BITSER ranking to find out how the people in your target group(s) are spread across the six steps and which steps form the obstacles. You will require a separate BITSER ranking for each of your target groups. The six questions described in chapter law 3 are a handy tool for this. Don't worry about correct rankings at this stage. I describe how to check your BITSER ranking in the chapter on law 6. On the next page is an example of a BITSER ranking for celebrity-chef Jamie Oliver's famous restaurant.

B	6	Awareness of the restaurant name is the smallest obstacle. Customers not spontaneously recommend the brand is the largest (Referral sales).
I	5	
T	3	
S	2	
E	4	
R	1	

B INSUFFICIENT BRAND AWARENESS

I BRAND IS NOT CONSIDERED

T VISITS TO SALE LOCATION OR APPOINTMENTS ARE TOO INFREQUENT

S VISITORS TO THE SALES LOCATION DON'T BUY

E EXISTING CUSTOMERS DON'T CONTINUE TO BUY OR THEY LEAVE

R EXISTING CUSTOMERS ARE UNSUCCESSFUL IN RECOMMENDING YOU TO THEIR CONTACTS

HOW TO AVOID INCORRECT BITSER RANKINGS

I must emphasise that when you create a ranking you must not do this from the point of view of your own problem situation. It often happens that, when sales are down, an organisation reacts by giving the sales step the highest rank – this being the problem they want to quickly solve. This is wrong. And will lead to the wrong action being taken. A step only justifies a high rank once the people on it do not take action. In other words, the Sales step only justifies a higher rank when those on the Traffic step don't convert to buying.

On the other hand, if substantial numbers of people visit a store (so they were already on the Traffic step, as they have taken action) and also buy, no sales obstacle is present and the sales step is then gets a low ranking. If eight out of ten people buy, is there a sales problem?

No. However, these sales may still be too low. This is not because people are not buying – so there still isn't a sales problem – but because too few people are visiting the store. The Traffic step wil then get a high ranking and, as a result, traffic will be the problem that is addressed – and not sales.

BITSER ranking for special target groups
If you have to deal with special target groups, as in personnel recruitment or behavioural change, adapt the question using core elements, as described in the section on 'core elements of other target groups'.

You can create a BITSER ranking for the most diverse groups of people. How about that large group of people to whom you have to present tomorrow? If you rank them you will know which step(s) to focus your presentation on tomorrow. So you can tailor-make the presentation. And what of that one potential customer that you really want to attract, on which step is she/he positioned? And that job interview ... you really want the job! Create a BITSER ranking of the persons with whom you will be talking and you will soon be on your way to getting it. Redundancy cuts threatening? Create a BITSER ranking of those who decide your fate and significantly reduce the chances of your redundancy - because you will know how to deal with each of them. Regardless of the party or parties you're dealing with, you can always do a BITSER ranking to figure out which obstacles (BITSER steps) you need to focus on.

THE FORGOTTEN TARGET GROUP

There is another group that may not escape your attention.
These are the influencers.
They play no direct role in delivering financial gain, but do play a role in influencing and convincing those who directly generate your turnover.
Your 'paying public' are influenced by their environment – for instance by colleagues or family.
Create a BITSER ranking for these influencers too. Bear in mind that the paying customer is still the primary focus for your messages.
However, the influencers always receive less attention an may never dominate in this regard.

The whole organisation
Without your and your organisation's help, nobody can climb the steps. Did you know that everyone in your organisation - and in any with which you work - is consciously or unconsciously already ascending one of these six steps? You can distribute your entire organisation across the six steps. Everything in your organisation revolves around these steps. For proof just look around you - at what your people are doing. It's phenomenal. The BITSER stair is your organisation - and it's essential for your success.

Results translated into a BITSER activity plan, with priorities

The numbers of the BITSER ranking indicate the contribution made by the relevant steps to the obstacles that hamper achievement of your continuity goal. The step ranked 1 thus presents the biggest obstacle. And the step ranked 6 the smallest.

The numbers 1, 2 and 3 constitute the vast majority of the problems. They create your real problems. They pose the biggest risks to achieving your turnover target - and thus to the continuity of your organisation. They demand top priority, direct action and lots of attention!

The other steps, ranked 4, 5 and 6, complete the system. They are less problematic than the first three. By engaging them you extract even more from your target group, in order to achieve your continuity turnover goal, and in reality, often a little bit more.

AN INTERNAL BITSING PLAN IS ESSENTIAL

An internal plan based on the Bitsing method as essential for the organisation's staff. Employees, after all, are responsible for everything that happens in the organisation. If they don't perform well it becomes difficult to make a profit. They must also climb the six BITSER steps in order to get to the point at which they can optimise their contribution to the achievement of the objectives. A properly functioning internal organisation means the battle for success is already half won.

Describing and prioritising the obstacles

After analysing the ranking you can draw conclusions and, on the basis of these, draft a plan of action. The first part of the action plan provides insight into the obstacles and the order of priority of the BITSER steps. The descriptions of the obstacles on the BITSER stair are:

B INSUFFICIENT BRAND AWARENESS

I BRAND IS NOT CONSIDERED

T TOO LITTLE OR NO VISITS TO SALE LOCATION; OR NO APPOINTMENTS

S VISITORS TO THE SALES LOCATION DON'T BUY

E EXISTING CUSTOMERS ARE NOT RET DO NOT CARRY ON BUYING

R EXISTING CUSTOMERS ARE UNSUCCESSF IN SELLING YOU TO THEIR CONTACTS

The BITSER ranking shows which obstacles dominate in the target group and which are present to a lesser degree. Your target group obstacles are in clear view.

The activity mix
The six BITSER stair steps, ask for six activities. These activities in turn guide the specific actions required to assist people to advance to the next step. The second part of the activity plan is to specify what the six activities are and the order of priority in which you will address them. They are:

B BUILDING BRAND AWARENESS AMONG THOSE WHO DON'T KNOW THE BRAND NAME

I IMAGE PROFILING FOR THOSE WHO NOT CONSIDER THE BRAND

T TRAFFIC GENERATION AMONG THOSE WHO DO NOT VISIT THE SALES LOCATION

S SALES STIMULATION AMONG THOSE NOT BUYING THE PRODUCT OR SERVICE

E EXTRA SALES STIMULATION FOR THOSE WHO DON'T CONTINUE TO BUY ALL YOUR ORGANISATION HAS TO OFFER THEM

R REFERRAL SALES - TO ACTIVATE THOSE WHO DO NOT SUCCESSFULLY SELL TO THEIR CONTACTS

THE ACTIVITY MIX

B ESTABLISH BRAND AWARENESS

I COMMUNICATE BRAND IMAGE

T ACHIEVE TRAFFIC IN SALES LOCATIONS

S STIMULATE PRODUCT SALES

E STIMULATE EXTRA SALES

R PROMOTE REFERRAL SALES

A BITSER activity plan always consists of a mix of activities, aimed at he corresponding personal profile, each with its own priorities. Now look at the ranking you compiled. Which three activities have the highest priority? And which of the three steps present a significantly lower priority? Also identify the personal profile you will encounter the most - and the profile that will present you with the least problems.

What happens if someone is targeted with the wrong activity? Nothing! To what extent are you willing to have a conversation with a sales-person who wants to promote a brand that you don't want? Or to test drive a car - if you already have that make of car? Select activities of high priority and which fit the relevant personal profile. This will ensure that you talk about the right things - and that you will succeed.

A tip!

Everything changes after you've engaged a target group. Nothing stays the same - because you are, after all, actively working to eradicate the obstacles. A BITSER ranking will therefore also change over time. A BITSER step currently forming the biggest obstacle in a target group, will, in time, no longer be the biggest obstacle. Another step will become that and you will point your activities in that direction. In this way all BITSER steps will get other positions in the ranking. Periodic analysis using BITSER ranking is important, to see if an activity plan still applies to the actual problems that prevail in a target group. Make adjustments if the ranking changes. One of the strengths of the Bitsing method is that it always uses actual facts. Recalibrate the BITSER ranking.

A thing about the classical approach to target groups is that it's just not the best way. However, the good news is that if you have been clinging to the classical approach you have a potential opportunity: you could perform 300% better in this area! In the classical approach an organisation will repeatedly use the same marketing campaign on a particular target group. This repeated use of the same campaign, which in no way covers all the steps of the BITSER stair, means that the results will never represent the full potential of that target group.

Equally characteristic of the classical approach is that communication stops completely following each campaign. In these silent periods there is obviously no communication - and goals are consequently not achieved. The following case study shows how communication becomes much more effective when based on the six steps of the BITSER model.

An educational institution must recruit students in order to achieve its turnover goal. Recruited students are recorded by date. The chart shows the number of recruited students by month and week. The top row shows the number of students recruited via conventional activity. The second row shows the results of the following year - in which the Bitsing method was applied and the campaigns were structured according to the BITSER model.

Classic vs. MODERN

	JUNE				JULY				AUGUST					SEPTEMBER				OCTOBER				NOV
WEEK NO.	23	24	25	26	27	28	29	30	31	32	33	34	35	36	37	38	39	40	41	42	43	44
YEAR OF CONVENTIONAL MARKETING	38	31	34	20	19	16	22	18	19	13	25	27	27	27	33	18	14	18	29	15	19	22
PRECEDING YEAR OF BITSING (BLUE)	30	28	36	30	31	22	18	28	22	20	35	51	38	57	48	27	37	33	37	14	26	26
DIFFERENCE IN RESULTS	-8	-3	+2	+10	+12	+6	-4	+10	+3	+7	+10	+24	+11	+30	+15	+9	+23	+15	+8	-1	+7	14
NON-BITSING WEEKS																						

All the periods in which Bitsing was applied show growth. More students were recruited in the year of Bitsing application than in the previous year, in which conventional methods were applied. Growth was not seen, however, in weeks 23, 24, 29 and 42, in which the school did worse than in the previous year. The reason for this is interesting. The first 'bad weeks' — week 23 and 24 — were still subject to the conventional approach, in which a single campaign was repeated. In comparison, six campaigns (in line with the six BITSER steps) were used in the successful weeks – 25, 26, 27 and 28. The result was growth. In week 29, however, there is a decline. The number of recruited students is lower. What happened? Well, the school stopped the six BITSER activities in week 29 in order to work on its website. This cannot be allowed to happen. Bitsing 'law' requires ongoing communication, using six BITSER executions. Weeks 30 to 41 accordingly reflect outstanding results, some weeks showing growth of more than 100%. But not week 42. In that week the number of recruited students again dropped, to a level below that of the preceding year. I was pleased to hear that this was not due to the application of Bitsing methodology! The school had again stopped the campaign, 'Because no one responds in the Autumn vacation'. Nonsense, in Bitsing terms ... keep on communicating! And indeed, with communication resumed, the remaining weeks all showed growth.

THE CONCLUSION

COMMUNICATE AND YOU WILL ACHIEVE YOUR GOAL!

CONSISTENLY APPLY THE STEPS OF THE BITSER MODEL - AND GROWTH WILL ENSUE. AND DON'T STOP TO SEE WHAT HAPPENS, YOU'LL STOP GROWING.

LAW 5

ONLY DEPLOY
EFFECTIVE
PROCESSES
AND
PROGRAMMES

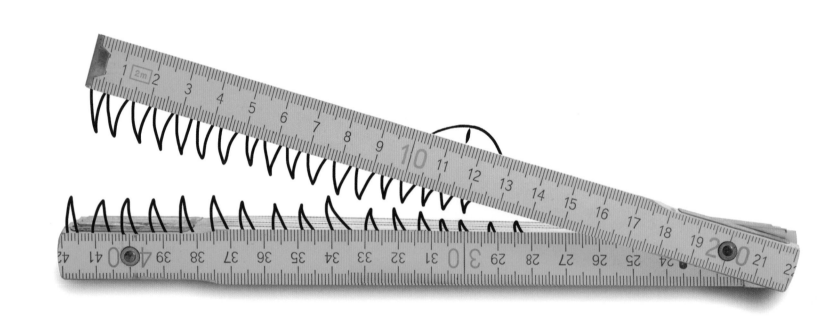

A FOCUSED MESSAGE GETS A LISTENING AUDIENCE

One of the wisest lessons I've learnt is from the world's leading business school, Wharton University in Pennsylvania: 'There are three reasons why good strategies fail - implementation, implementation and implementation'. You can make the best plans, but poor execution will deliver a debacle. It took me many years before I realised what good implementation of a plan actually requires. Throughout my career I have been involved in the development and implementation of hundreds of business plans, marketing plans, communication plans, financial plans, organisational plans and of course 'Bitsing plans'. I have learned a huge amount and will share this knowledge with you.

In this chapter I'll deal with the secrets for successful implementation of your Bitsing plan and, as part of that, your BITSER activity plan. You will discover the most powerful ways of transforming the words of your plan into successful activities.

The only thing a Bitsing plan does not do
Your entire organisation will get involved in the execution of your Bitsing plan - and yet it won't add to anyone's workload. Which is the only thing that a Bitsing plan won't do! It's almost self-completing, in particular because it is so obvious. I can promise you that it will save anyone a lot of time, without hampering growth in any way. It will inspire and motivate them - and your (potential)

customers - and all the other people in your target groups."Bitsing remains impressive in its simplicity and accuracy", says Sven Kramer, one of the strategy leaders in one of the world's largest companies, Shell International. And yet it is a complete business plan, which explains everything that is needed and exposes the information needed to achieve your goal. Whether you work alone or with tens of thousands of employees, it is now clear to you that they need only concern themselves with six activities to ensure the continuity of your organisation. How efficiently can you guide and lead your organisation if you only need to focus on six clear activities? And how effectively will you execute the activities if there are so few of them? An effectiveness improvement of tens of per cent is the rule rather than the exception, according to the experiences of many Bitsing users. As are spontaneous savings in time, non-performing resources and money. A saving of over 25% is highly likely, as a result of the right focus, attention and operation. Read on, as we will lay the foundation for the perfect way to set up your organisation (regardless of its format) and implement the required activities.

Always: a mix of programme activities
When rolling out a plan based on the Bitsing method you will never have only one, dominant focus on a single dominant issue. Your entire organisation will work on six different activities, engaging the famous steps of the BITSER stair. Every step requires its own activity, otherwise the people on the stair will not progress and you will not reach your goal. You'll always therefore be implementing a mix of six activities. Call them programmes from now on - because an activity is not something that you just do once. Offering your products or services only once will not entice people to buy them - to mention just one example.

You're going to launch external programmes to entice the target groups on whom your continuity turnover goal depends. And you'll launch internal programmes aimed at your employees and colleagues with whom you will achieve your goals. Who, in fact, will achieve your goals for you.

Each of the BITSER programmes is tasked with effectively completing its work, namely helping people on one step of the BITSER stair to progress a step further. This is easier to do than it appears. To help someone climb to the next step you should only focus on one issue. Explanation: If the first step of the BITSER model, step B, is about knowing the name of your brand or organisation, then you only need to make sure the target group knows your name - and no more than that. This is the simple approach for each BITSER step and each related programme. You focus on only one issue per step, with the task of helping the target audience on that step of the stair to take the next step.

I'll now set out the criteria for effective preparation and implementation of the programmes. Your continuity target is almost achieved!

THE SIX BITSER PROGRAMMES

B ESTABLISH AWARENESS

I CREATE BRAND PREFERENCE

T TRAFFIC AT POINT OF SALE

S ACHIEVE PRODUCT SALES

E STIMULATE EXTRA SALES

R STIMULATE REFERRAL

CRITERION 1 EXECUTE YOUR POLICY USING SIX PROGRAMMES
In chapter 3 I spoke extensively about the three types of policies for removing all the barriers that stand in the way of your continuity goal. You execute these policies using the six BITSER programmes.

The B and I programmes are for execution of the brand preference policy.

The T and S programmes actualise the product of service buying behaviour policy.

The E and R programmes are there to implement the organisation loyalty policy.

CRITERION 2 FOLLOW THE PROGRAMME STRATEGY

You can only spend your money once - and the deployment of your people, the investment of your own time and the attention you can give are also limited to just 100%. Yet you will have to execute six programmes. Which means that any single programme will never get 100% of your attention. You will need to divide that attention between the six programmes. The Bitsing method expresses this allocation of attention in percentages. This is called 'the programme strategy'.

Allocating attention percentages

In order to calculate programme focus percentages we must go back to chapters 3 and 4, in which I explained how you create a BITSER ranking and convert the ranking into focus percentages. Read it one more time if you need to refresh your memory. Each digit in the BITSER ranking stands for a focus percentage: 1 = 30%; 2 = 25%; 3 = 20%; 4 = 15%; 5 = 10% and 6 = 5%. You can now assign the focus percentages to the programmes. The programme with the highest ranking gets the highest focus percentage (i.e. 30%), and lowest in ranking gets the lowest percentage (5%). This reveals a programme's share of the activities.

AN EXAMPLE :

B	PROGRAMME 4	15%
I	PROGRAMME 1	30%
T	PROGRAMME 5	10%
S	PROGRAMME 3	20%
E	PROGRAMME 2	25%
R	PROGRAMME 6	5%

The ranking indicates a programme's priority; the percentages of attention form the programme strategy.
In this example the I programme gets the highest priority and the most attention, namely 30%. The R programme requires the least attention, namely 5%. The other programmes are in between. The percentages indicate the level of attention you should pay to a programme.

What does percentage of attention mean?
'Attention' has many meanings.

IN THE FIRST PLACE: 'dedication'.
The percentage indicates a programme's share of all activities. If the S programme has a share of 20%, then no more than

FROM BITSER RANKING TO PROGRAMME STRATEGY

PROGRAMME	RANKING 1	30	PERCENT FOCUS
PROGRAMME	RANKING 2	25	PERCENT FOCUS
PROGRAMME	RANKING 3	20	PERCENT FOCUS
PROGRAMME	RANKING 4	15	PERCENT FOCUS
PROGRAMME	RANKING 5	10	PERCENT FOCUS
PROGRAMME	RANKING 6	5	PERCENT FOCUS

THE TOTAL OF PERCENTAGES IS 105% DUE TO ROUNDING

20% of what your organisation does should focus on sales. A single programme can never have a larger share than 30% of all of your programmes. This is the highest possible percentage. Whatever problems you have to deal with, whatever challenges await you, and even though your instinct may tell you differently, a programme should never, never, never have a greater share in the activities of your organisation than 30%! A larger share will not increase the results that you extract from your target group.

SECONDLY: 'alertness'. As the percentage of a programme is higher, its importance, in terms of your success, increases. The higher its percentage, the more critically you should check the correctness of a programme's content.

THIRDLY: 'concentration'. You should concentrate particularly on programmes with the highest percentages. Only look at the three highest percentages, 30, 25 and 20. And if you add them up? The total of these three percentages is 75. Do you know what that means? That if you focus only on the three programmes with the highest percentages, you will overcome 75% of the obstacles in your market and target audience.

WHAT IS YOUR ORGANISATION CURRENTLY DOING?

WICH OF THE FOLLOWING ACTIVITIES RECIEVE MORE THAN 40%* OF YOUR ORGANISATION'S ATTENTION (IN TERMS OF ENERGY, TIME, MONEY AND PEOPLE)?

- o SALES
- o COST SAVING
- o SOLVING PROBLEMS
- o CUSTOMER RETENTION
- o PERSONAL RECRUITMENT
- o PRODUCT DEVELOPMENT
- o MARKETING
- o LEAN
- o INTERNAL MOTIVATION
- o PRODUCTION
- o OTHER:

* WICH IS FAR TOO MUCH. 30% IS THE MAXIMUM!

What it also says is that if you only work with a single programme - for example the programme with the highest share, 30% - then 70% of the people in your target market will not be affected and 70% of your obstacles will not be resolved. Focusing on a single problem thus has no effect.

FOURTHLY 'money'. What I tend to do is to use the percentages of the programmes as a guide to spending on the programmes. Suppose you have 100 euros to spend, then 30 euros go to the programme with the largest percentage share (30% of 100 euros), 25 euros will go to the next programme, and so on. The percentages of the programme strategy are an extremely enlightening tool when it comes to committing your budget, helping you not to spend too much and not to spend erroneously.

The perfection of the programme strategy
The percentages of the programme strategy are actually the advance messengers of your target market, telling you what people need from you, regardless of whether they are inside or outside your organisation. The percentages indicate the intensity with which you help every person in your target market to ascend the steps of the BITSER stair in the fastest way.

Pushing too hard by giving too much attention to a step, or pushing too little, does not help people make any progress at all.

To each programme its own effect
Be aware that no programme has or should have the same effect as another. Only when you aim the right programme at someone, can it do its job effectively and help that person ascend a step further on the BITSER stair. Understanding that the six steps of the BITSER stair are different from each other will lead you to the knowledge that each of the BITSER programmes has to comply with different, specific requirements. Otherwise they will not be effective. The S programme, aimed at selling your product, does little for awareness - but does sell your product. Conversely, a B programme – aimed at building awareness – does not sell, but does bring the necessary awareness. So it goes, for each of the six programmes. They each have their own, specific requirements.

CRITERION 3 ALLOCATE TASKS TO PROGRAMMES - NOT OBJECTIVES
Give someone a goal and they may not know how to achieve it. Give someone a task and the goal will be achieved. Suppose I have a dry throat and need water. I say to my personal assistant: 'I'd like to wet my throat.' Anything could appear on my desk - including, maybe, water. However, if I make it a task: 'Please will you get me a glass of water?' – water will arrive. Each of the programmes in the BITSER activity plan – and therefore also the people participating in the programme - have a task which leads to achievement of the goal.

The task of the B programme is to attract attention. After all, without attention there's no awareness. The task of the I programme is to be irresistible. To create want or preference. The T programme's task is to activate. Without action people do not get into motion. The task of the S programme is to be convincing. Without conviction there will be no purchase. The task of the E programme is retention. If someone is not retained there is not much more to gain from them. Finally, the task of the R programme is to bind; someone who is bound to you does everything for you, including reselling to his personal contacts.

CRITERION 4 ALWAYS CHOOSE THE RIGHT SUBJECT
Each of the six programmes deals with a separate subject. The B programme concerns the name of your brand or organisation. It should be known, i.e. it must enjoy brand awareness.

The I programme gives meaning to the name. The associations with this name constitute the brand - the thing 'I want'. The T programme has as its subject the place where one buys - the sales location, the point of sale. One could also say, the distribution channel. And people will have to go to it in order for us to proceed to S. The S programme concerns the product or service that people should, and consequently do, buy. The E programme contains all the other products and services of your organisation. The programme is operative in the internal organisation, which supports the products and services. The R programme supports the relationship with the customer, which binds people to your organisation.

These notions should be familiar and clearly recognisable, both to the people in your organisation who work with them (internal programme) and to the receivers in your target audience (external programme).

CRITERION 5
DON'T TALK NONSENSE
Non-sense. Words that mean nothing. Yet before we know it we're using them, chattering meaninglessly. Calling someone a client when they're not - is nonsense. Attempting to sell something to someone before the brand name is known -

is nonsense. Trying to build awareness using sales techniques - is nonsense. Telling a loyal customer how good your brand is - is nonsense. He already knows. Marketing programmes that 'talk nonsense' communicate in a way that is irrelevant to the listener. This irrelevance occurs when a programme is built on the application of incorrect messages and techniques. Each of the six BITSER programmes has its own set of "technical" criteria. Applying the wrong criteria has the wrong effect. The programme will be destructive instead of constructive. What we will do next is learn how to apply the right techniques to the right BITSER programme, and avoid talking nonsense.

Effective programmes in an efficient organisation
What follows is an insider's view of the technical 'tricks' of the BITSER programmes. These will enable you to create programmes that don't just help a little - they will help you to succeed completely, reap the maximum reward - and achieve your continuity turnover target!

1 BASIC TECHNIQUES OF THE B PROGRAMME
B programme techniques are used to establish a brand name. Your brand must be 'out there' and it must be (better) known.

This requires the attention of your target group. Without it, awareness will not follow. But you have to claim this attention. It doesn't come automatically – it is the task of the people you involve in this programme and in the resulting marketing programme. Attention comes from standing out. The element of surprise makes you stand out best - and the B programme is surprising. In fact that is its main characteristic. The nature of the external campaigns that support this programme is best formulated as 'short and sweet'. Check the focus percentages of your programme strategy (see beginning of this chapter) to find out exactly how much attention this programme must get.

2 BASIC TECHNIQUES OF THE I PROGRAMME
The I programme gives weight to the brand, it gives the brand significance. This is generated and achieved using the emotional propositions of your brand (see the preference strategy in law 3). The I programme must make the brand special - and the market must appreciate just how special it is. It must, after all, be the most appealing brand in existence. Remember the uncopyability factor (the golden egg)? What other brand has that? Only yours. And the market must get to know this.

So be dynamic in activating your brand. Touch the emotions and (as a result) position the brand. A static approach makes your brand boring. You can also radiate authority - after all, you're invincible. This is a powerful advantage in leveraging both staff motivation and the achieving the desired positive effects among your external audience. Finally, avoid arrogance. This negative characteristic won't benefit your brand and, accordingly, has no role as a BITSER technique. Who works on the I programme? It's often your marketing team.

3 BASIC TECHNIQUES OF THE T PROGRAMME

The T programme is focused on the sales location. Its job is, literally, to get your target group in motion - towards the sales location at which the purchase will eventually take place. The location could be a store, a web shop, a mobile phone, a salesperson - any location at which a sale can be concluded. When 'behaviour change' is being 'sold', for instance in a road safety campaign aimed at car drivers, the sales location is the car. It is the place where the change of behaviour has to be 'bought' or implemented. People rarely set themselves in motion. The barriers that obstruct the desired behaviour should first be removed. This is easily done using a risk-free ('non-commercial') activity or action offer, which in no way relate to your product or service and do not appear to be 'selling'. The T programme, after all, is not about your product or service, but about the distribution channel, the sales location. The 'risk-free' offer of a test drive in a car, for example, is actually high-risk, because we all know that it is meant to sell the car. When your (sales) team develops and launches your risk-free activity/sales location offer allow these externally targeted campaigns to be refreshingly 'non-commercial' and unforced. Fling open your doors and lower the thresholds to action!

4 BASIC TECHNIQUES OF THE S PROGRAMME

In this programme you're working with the actual product or service. This is, in fact, about your product and sales strategies; they cover the area from development and innovation of your product up to its marketing and delivery. And they use and deploy the rational propositions of your product or service (see law 3). 'Product sale' here has a broader meaning. It includes the 'sale' of desired behaviours to employees, successfully selling your organisation to the right job applicant, convincing a celebrity to speak at your conference and so on. This is the only programme in which product and service are discussed. In all other programmes the very mention of these words is forbidden. The percentages of the (earlier described) programme strategy will indicate exactly how much attention to pay to this product or service programme, with regard to both internal and external target groups.The S programme basically forces the purchasing decision. Postponing the decision increases the risk of failing to purchase. So when people enter the sales location (which they will do, thanks to the effects of the T programme described left) - it's now or never. The purchase decision happens quicker if the consideration time is shortened.

You do this by not letting people reflect a lot about the product or service in its entirety, but focus more on the rational proposition of the product (see purchasing behaviour strategy, law 3) and the deal you're offering them. The technique of not pushing the product or service during the sale, but focusing on the rational arguments and offering a deal, obviously accelerates the purchase decision. People also want to have the feeling that they've achieved something in the negotiation preceding the sale. The best way to create this feeling is to develop and offer a value benefit that has a direct connection with the product or service. Everyone recognises value - and enjoys receiving it. The most basic value offer is a discount - and is to be avoided. It will always cost you and affect your margin. There are very many ways to provide your potential customer with a value advantage, at extremely low cost. Limited time offers will push people to decide more quickly. These offers work well in your Sales campaigns. One business generated twice its normal turnover through a typo in its campaign copy: The company had a special offer, which was valid for thirty days. A typographical error shortened the thirty days to three. Instead of 'This offer is valid for 30 days', the copy read, 'This offer is valid for 3 days'.

The short duration of the offer resulted in a literal run on the stores. So they decided to have a major promotion entitled, 'Three crazy days' on an annual basis. It's now in its 20th successful year. Limited time offers have greater effect in the consumer market than in the business market. The business market often involves longer decision periods and larger amounts of money. The external campaigns for this programme should be commercial and hard selling, for both consumer and business markets. Your aim, after all, is to force a decision.

5 BASIC TECHNIQUES OF THE E PROGRAMME

The E programme is about additional sales - over and above what the customer has already bought from you. This doesn't come easily. Your purchaser – the customer - must be satisfied before he will buy more. Dissatisfaction stops further action. Extra sales are created from a palette of relational propositions, as described in law 3. All the extras your business has to offer can be used to add 'extra sales' value to the products that you sold under the S programme. Make the value of these extras very clear to your existing customers and you will retain them on this basis. Retention of the customer is your primary mission.

So set up a programme that will value the customer. Someone who feels valued is easier to retain. A valued person is a satisfied person. Appreciate your customers - give them an unconditional reward. Don't require an extra purchase. Give it because you appreciate the customer. It's a benefit for the customer, not for the business. You're giving something to the customer (valuing him), instead of wanting something from him (selling). It's a gesture, a gift, a reward - 'just because you're our customer'. There are many kinds of free extras. Arrange an event, hold 'knowledge sessions' with clients - these are also rewards. Nothing is 'sold', but people will still end up buying. The benefit you offer should be useful and non-commercial. Let this also determine the tone of your external campaigns. The very way in which you present the programme must say you are there for the customer.

6 BASIC TECHNIQUES OF THE R PROGRAMME

The R programme builds relationships with the loyal users of your product. It encourages them to recommend your products and services to their personal circle - to your benefit, for new customers are introduced. Customers will do this because they have become loyal. And loyalty is something that grows between people. Which is why your (client service) staff play the leading roles in this programme and why relational propositions are effective here as well. Loyalty comes from two sides. You ask the customer to do something for you, namely acquire new customers. And you give something in return - recognition of the relationship with the customer. (For instance by perhaps introducing him to a new client - from your network?) People who feel accepted and recognised are more likely to become loyal. The best form of recognition is to involve the customer in your organisation: you need him and he needs you. The essence of this programme is the creation of a personal bond between your customers and your staff and which will continue into the future.

If your BITSER programmes meet their technical criteria, they will do their job effectively.

PROGRAMME TECHNIQUES

B BITSER PROGRAMME

TARGET PERSON PROFILE>
SUSPECTS
SUBJECT> BRAND OR ORGANISATION NAME
TASK> GENERATE ATTENTION
STRATEGY> GET NOTICED
EXECUTION> SURPRISING
METHOD> SHORT & SHARP

>>>>> B <<<<<<<<<<<<<

I BITSER PROGRAMME

TARGET PERSON PROFILE>
POTENTIALS
SUBJECT> NATURE OF BRAND OR ORGANISATION
TASK> BECOME UNBEATABLE
STRATEGY> BEING UNBEATABLE
PROPOSITION> EMOTIONAL
EXECUTION> UNCOPYABILITY FACTOR
METHOD> DYNAMIC AND DOMINANT

>>>> I <<<<<<<<<<<<

T BITSER PROGRAMME

TARGET PERSON PROFILE>
PREFERRERS
SUBJECT> SALES LOCATION
TASK> ACTIVATE
STRATEGY> REMOVE OBSTACLES TO ACTION
EXECUTION> RISK-FREE
METHOD NON-COMMERCIAL AND UNFORCED

>>>>> T <<<<<<<<<<<<

← NOT PRODUCT OR SERVICE LINKED

S BITSER PROGRAMME

TARGET PERSON PROFILE>
MOVERS
SUBJECT> PRODUCT OR SERVICE
TASK> FORCE DECISION
STRATEGY> A DEAL
PROPOSITION> RATIONAL
APPROACH> SELLING
AND COMMERCIAL
◎◎◎◎◎◎ METHOD> TEMPORARY, VALUABLE

>>>> S <<<<<<<<<< <<

← SHARP PENC
SEE LAW 2

← PRODUCT OR
SERVICE
LINKED

E BITSER PROGRAMME

TARGET PERSON PROFILE>
BUYERS
SUBJECT> THE ORGANISATION, TOGETHER
WITH ITS OTHER PRODUCTS AND SERVICES
TASK> RETAIN
STRATEGY> APPRECIATE THE CUSTOMER/BUYER
PROPOSITION> RELATIONAL
EXECUTION> OBLIGATION-FREE REWARD
◎◎◎◎◎◎ APPROACH> SERVICE-ORIENTED & GIVING

>>>> E <<<<<<<<<<<< <<

← WITHOUT
WANTING
ANYTHING
IN
RETURN

R BITSER PROGRAMME

TARGET PERSON PROFILE>

USERS
SUBJECT> RELATIONSHIP
TASK> LOYALTY
STRATEGY> RECOGNISE THE RELATIONSHIP
EXECUTION> INVOLVES INTERNAL ORGANISATION
◎◎◎◎◎◎ APPROACH> TOGETHER, BONDING

>>>> R <<<<<<<<<< <<

CRITERION 6 MAKE SURE YOU ARE SEEN - BECAUSE SEEING IS BELIEVING

You can have the best programme, but if it's not received by your target group it's all been for nothing. This counts for external and internal programmes. The effects of your internal programmes should also be seen and felt by your external target group. Only then do they have positive effect. Your BITSER programme is carried and communicated by a medium – that could be a person...the employee working in the programme; it could also be some other medium that communicates with the people in your target market. Ultimately, everything with which you can reach your external and internal target markets is a means and a medium of communication. This could include, for instance, the facade of your building and, of course, your advertising content and the media channels that carry it.

Unless you yourself are the medium, you have no personal influence on whether your targeted people are reached by other media. For this reason your BITSER programmes use the means and media best suited to achieving their specific goals - and maximising their chances of being noticed. For example, someone who doesn't want your brand will show no interest in a retail shop sales promotion displaying your products.

Means and media have individual and specific characteristics

You can drive a screw into a wall with a hammer, but you'll get the best results with a screwdriver. The same applies to the means, content and media used in your BITSER programmes.

While every medium may possess some flexibility, each will also have its strongest feature. If you recognise and use this key feature you can make your programme more effective. In other words, apply media to the programme where they work best. Is an employee who cannot sell the right person to choose to run an S programme? If your ad is hidden somewhere on page 43 of a magazine will it build your awareness and therefore be a suitable choice for your B programme? No. Yet media are often randomly selected - for reasons like individual preference, individual financial interest, or simply because things have not been thought through properly.

BITSER programmes have specific media requirements

There are more than sixty available media types. And they are increasing in number. Which means it's not easy to make choices. I will demonstrate that the medium itself is not so important, but rather its characteristics.

The type of BITSER programme determines which media characteristics are required - i.e. those best able to assist a target person to climb the next step. These required media characteristics determine, in turn, which medium is chosen. Below is a list of programmes by their appropriate media characteristics. I call this the media strategy.

Key media characteristics, matched to the programmes they fit best:

B	PROGRAMME	**B**	MEDIA	TEASING
I	PROGRAMME	**I**	MEDIA	POSITIONING
T	PROGRAMME	**T**	MEDIA	ACTIVATING
S	PROGRAMME	**S**	MEDIA	CONVINCING
E	PROGRAMME	**E**	MEDIA	SATISFYING
R	PROGRAMME	**R**	MEDIA	RELATIONAL

1 CHARACTERISTICS OF B MEDIA
TEASING

These media are effective in the context of the B programme because they have impact and can attract attention. Stimulating media will be relevant to and 'cover' the majority of a target group. This is because these media are rather general by nature - but very effectively attract attention. It is difficult for their audience to 'avoid' them and they are also not easily displaced by competing stimuli in the environment. Hardly anything will be able to distract attention from your message. A teasing medium can achieve great effect in a short period of time (though for this very reason is effective only in the short term).

B MEDIA CHARACTERISTICS
- a - MASS
- b - UNAVOIDABLE
- c - FLEETING, FAST
- d - NO NOISE

2 CHARACTERISTICS OF I MEDIA
POSITIONING

Positioning media are effective in the context of the I programme because of their dynamic ability to stir the emotions. Positioning media are selective and 'emotive'. Capable of expressing/stimulating emotion and conveying (emotive) images. These media must be matched to a clearly defined target group, consisting of people with a particular profile. The positioning medium must also fit the personality of your brand. If your brand is for golfers choose a Golf TV programme or golf magazine. If your brand fits accountants select the medium that reaches this group. Positioning media also often have a social 'position'. They may have authority - often coupled with subscription to a magazine title, a digital TV channel, etc. As with teasing media, positioning media can have a big effect in a short period of time.

I MEDIA CHARACTERISTICS
- a - SELECTIVELY DEPLOYABLE
- b - CAPABLE OF CONVEYING IMAGES
- c - DYNAMIC
- d - EMOTIVE

3 CHARACTERISTICS OF T MEDIA
ACTIVATING

The media best suited to the T programme provide the opportunity for a direct response. Activating media are directly aimed at the target group member - and are tangible. Activating media are not personal in the sense of 'knowing' the target person's identity, but they do communicate in such a way that individuals feel personally addressed. And they can reach an exact number of people - something that is virtually impossible to achieve with the previous two media types, which are aimed at groups. Activating media 'take you by the hand'. They work in the personal environment, generate a physical response and are directly accessible. There is no separation between you and the medium, so you can interact with it. As these media present an opportunity to react your message should therefore include an opportunity to respond.

T MEDIA CHARACTERISTICS
- a - DIRECT
- b - (RE)ACTIVE
- c - RESPONSIVE
- d - ACCESSIBLE

4 CHARACTERISTICS OF S MEDIA
CONVINCING

These media are confrontational, fleeting and therefore well fitted to stimulating sales. They are impactful, persuasive and always found at the point of sale, near the product or service. These media are characterised by their temporarily nature. They are actually only relevant at the moment of the decision to purchase, when the transaction can actually be concluded.

Convincing media are therefore present at the moment and in the place where the deal is done. In other words in the store, or during the sales pitch.

S MEDIA CHARACTERISTICS
a - CONFRONTATIONAL
b - ON THE SPOT
c - TEMPORARY
d - AT THE MOMENT OF THE DEAL

5 CHARACTERISTICS OF E MEDIA
SATISFYING
The service-oriented character of these media means they are able to assist in the process of making the client feel valued. Satisfying media are personal and work within the personal environment of the recipient. Satisfying media are capable of communicating appreciation. These are media that bring something instead of taking it away. They are media that must be capable of being of service to the buyer. They are rewarding. And they are often generated from within the organisation and not from outside it. Helpdesks and customer outings are examples.

E MEDIA CHARACTERISTICS
a - PERSONAL
b - GIVING
c - SERVICE-ORIENTED
d - APPRECIATIVE

6 CHARACTERISTICS OF R MEDIA
RELATIONAL
R media are required for implementation of the R programme. They have a special capacity to connect and bind. Relational media are focused on the individual, but underline that the organisation and individual interact, do things together. They are therefore more like 'live entertainment' than a static medium. They 'entertain' because you can more easily ask your customer to help you when you are both in a neutral, non-commercial environment. The theatre, a football match, dinner and so on are examples - away from the business environment. These media strengthen the relationship with the customer, while keeping distance from your business relationship. This is about people and the bond between them, which these media can facilitate.

R MEDIA CHARACTERISTICS
a - INDIVIDUAL
b - INVOLVED
c - ENTERTAINING
d - TOGETHER

People and BITSER programmes
In many organisations people do work that they are actually not good at. They may seem to be suited to their position, if you look at their experience - but not if you look at who they are, inwardly. You can, however, set up your organisation or department to conform to the requirements of the BITSER model. Each step of the model represents a person. Look at the required techniques, per BITSER programme, described above. What type of person fits these requirements best? Numerous reorganisations have taken place based on the BITSER model. It is a number of years since the first retail chain was organised according to the requirements of the Bitsing method and BITSER model.

B PROGRAMME DEMANDS A PERSONALITY THAT STANDS OUT

I PROGRAMME DEMANDS AN IMPASSIONED PERSONALITY

T PROGRAMME DEMANDS A DOOR OPENER, WHO REMOVES OBSTACLES - NOT A SALESPERSON

S PROGRAMME DEMANDS AN EFFECTIVE SALESPERSON WHO CLOSES THE SALE

E PROGRAMME DEMANDS A SERVICE ORIENTED PERSON

R PROGRAMME DEMANDS A RELATIONSHIP SPECIALIST, PERSON TO PERSON

What type of person would you put behind the programme?

The B programme requires an impactful personality, the I programme an inspirer, the T programme requires a door opener, who lowers thresholds - but not a sales person. The latter is needed for the S programme - someone with sales in his blood and a hunger to close. The E programme requires a service-orientated person and, finally, the R programme needs a people person, a relationship builder. You are probably familiar with the 'hunters' and 'farmers' concept. The hunters are sales people, part of the T and S programmes; farmers are after-sales people and are at home in the E and R programmes. And in the B and I programmes? Here you will find the missionaries, paving the way.

B I THE MISSIONARIES

T S THE HUNTERS

E R THE FARMERS

Programme frequency

Programme frequency is the frequency with which you approach a person during the target period. It is the number of times you address the target group occupying a given BITSER step with an activity from the programme. Approaching a person more than once guarantees that your message will eventually reach them.

The guideline for the consumer market (B2C) is that if you carry out an activity four times, someone will receive your message once. A frequency of four represents a single contact, one hit! These are the guidelines for two other markets:

Business market B2B

2 = 1 A frequency of two messages gives one contact.

Internal market B2E (staff)

1 = 1 A frequency of one message gives one contact.

The programme strategy percentages indicate the frequency of a programme. Let's look at the frequency guideline for the consumer market (B2C). Every 5% of focus is equivalent to approaching someone four times; in other words a frequency of four, during the target period. In a target period of twelve months the person in the example below will be approached with a promotion or activity from the relevant programme once every quarter. The programme strategy therefore translates into a guideline for B2C programme frequency:

Three intensity strategies
The programme strategy not only says something about the frequency, but also the intensity of a programme. A programme requiring a lot of attention will have to be more intensive than a programme that only needs minimal attention.

There are three frequency strategies introductory, building and maintained.

Introductory intensity
Programmes requiring focus levels of 30 and 25% are given the introductory

Building intensity
Programmes with focus percentages of 20 and 15 require building intensity. Building intensity programmes take place over medium-length periods of time and are carried out with a moderate frequency.

Maintained intensity
The maintained approach is applied to programmes with focus percentages of 10 and 5. This is the least intensive approach to the target group. The programme is executed over a long period of time at a low frequency.

PROGRAMME STRATEGY PERIOD 12 MONTHS	FREQUENCY	TARGET
PROGRAMME FOCUS 30%	24 x	2x PER MONTH
PROGRAMME FOCUS 25%	20 x	2x PER FIVE WEEKS
PROGRAMME FOCUS 20%	16 x	1x PER THREE WEEKS
PROGRAMME FOCUS 15%	12 x	1x PER MONTH
PROGRAMME FOCUS 10%	8 x	2x PER QUARTER
PROGRAMME FOCUS 5%	4 x	1x PER QUARTER

Adjust the frequency relative to the market you are dealing with (e.g. a business or internal market).

approach. The primary obstacles in a target group are dealt with in a short period. Introductory intensity requires that a programme is carried out over a short period of time with high frequency.

The importance of the right timing
All sorts of things can happen en route to achieving your continuity target. Facts can change, so you need to shift the focus. It could also happen that in a certain period, say a month, circumstances result in your not achieving the required turnover. This shortfall will have to be recovered in the ensuing periods. This, in turn, requires that you intensify your BITSER activities. Sub-divide the period in which you want to achieve the continuity turnover target into periods of quarters, months, or - if you have a smaller, more flexible organisation - even weeks. During each sub-period roll out all six BITSER programmes. In doing so you are aiming at achieving the turnover target

for the relevant sub-period. As a result you will execute the six BITSER programmes a number of times. Using these shorter, sub-periods enables you to adjust better to changing, current situations. The shorter the consecutive BITSER periods are, the better your capacity to adjust.

Note that some time can pass between the first contact with a target person and the final purchase. This may be one day, but could also be months and sometimes even years when it comes to complex products and services. Keep this in mind when planning BITSER programmes. I've experienced a situation in which a start had to be made on B programme to achieve a sales target which was two years away - this being the time required from first contact to final order. This is not unusual in the business market, in which months may intervene between the first appointment and the signing of a contract. So one needs to start early with the initial programmes in order to achieve a revenue target within a given period.

Knowledge comes from books, experience comes from practice. I have, of course, tried to put as much of my experience in this book as possible, but it will never be enough to immediately turn you into an experienced 'Bitseter'. You will only become one through applying the Bitsing method in practice.

SO START CREATING OUR OWN PROGRAMMES NOW!

Build experience as quickly as possible

LAW 6

PREDICT THE RESULTS BEFORE YOU ROLL OUT YOUR PROGRAMMES

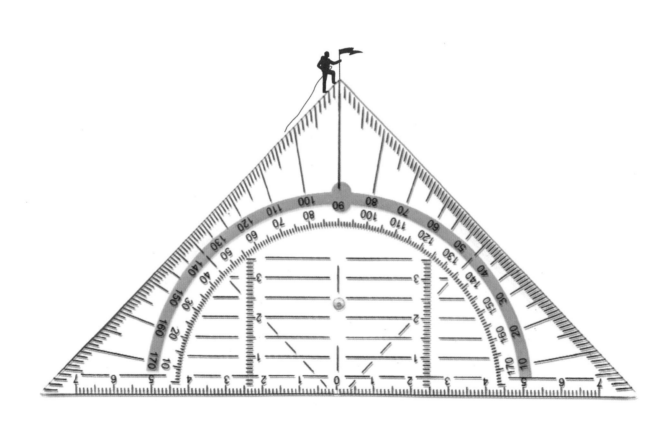

ISN'T IT GREAT WHEN YOU ALWAYS KNOW IN ADVANCE THAT YOU WILL ACHIEVE YOUR GOALS?

Once a year I visit a casino with a group of friends. It's part of a fun night out and we normally end the night in a restaurant and, of course, visit some of Amsterdam's delightful cafes. The interesting thing is that when we are in the restaurant no one sets a ceiling on budget. We select from the menu and later, when the bill arrives, we see what the meal cost. However, as soon as we enter the doors of the casino, we immediately set a maximum amount to wager. It seems that we assume that we will lose that amount anyway. What in fact is happening, is that we know what we will get in return for our money, in the restaurant - and in the casino we don't. The conclusion is compelling: if you do not know the result of your investment in advance, you will limit it to a maximum amount. If you do know in advance, it doesn't matter.

Organisations that impose limits on investment therefore do so because they do not know whether the investment will generate results. It is therefore significant that you know the results of your actions in advance. Otherwise you may unrealistically limit your budgets, or perhaps not invest at all. Which makes a 'win', to use the casino term, extremely doubtful. Advance knowledge of results is therefore critical to your success and - there you have it again - critical to achieving your continuity turnover goal!

Put it on 22!
Just imagine that my friends and I know in advance that a roulette ball will land on 22, a black number. What would we do? Exactly: put all our chips on black and 22. This is what the Bitsing method does for you: it predicts what will happen - the result of your programme activities. Bitsing cannot do this at the casino, because we unfortunately cannot influence the roulette wheel. But in your case - and that of your organisation as a whole - this is possible. To extend our casino metaphor - all you have to do now is move your hand to black and number 22 and place your chips there. Your 'hand' symbolises the programmes you will execute, the six BITSER programmes.

And from now on you will be able to do this on the basis of predicted outcomes.

Predicting the results

Using the Bitsing method to predict the results of your programme is an extraordinary process. And one with broad applications, for example predicting the results of the activities of a department, or of a marketing campaign, or of a series of telemarketing calls. The Bitsing method will predict sales team achievements, the performance of your employees, how many people will respond to your job offer, the number of shop visits, how many people will change their behaviour, the amount of increased customer spend and your increased turnover and profitability. Everything your organisation does is predictable in this sense, as long as it has to do with achieving your turnover continuity goal. And what of activities that do not serve this goal? I call those hobby activities: good for keeping you busy - if you need that - but unpredictable in the full sense of the word. As these activities lead nowhere.

Do nothing without first knowing the results

Advance knowledge of results means you'll be able to adapt and adjust as you go - and sleep peacefully.

The Bitsing method also excels in predicting when the required result will not be delivered. So when I predicted that a telecom company would lose 23% of their turnover in two months as the result of a badly conceived adaptation of their product strategy policy... it happened. I predicted that a railway company would, as a result of its decisions, suffer losses running into millions within a few years. And it happened. The predictive function of the Bitsing method helps prevent financial disasters. Above all, its ability to predict results, turnover and profit (see the definition of the method in the introduction) help to guarantee achievement of your continuity goal.

Playing snooker

You prepare the stroke by 'dummying' it, sliding the cue up and down, aiming, until the shot feels 'right' - and only then do you strike the ball. This is exactly what the Bitsing method does for you. It helps you get the angle and force of the stroke right, in advance. The difference between the Bitsing method and your feelings is that Bitsing relies on facts. As a result, you can hold the cue in exactly the right position - to the millimetre. And the right starting position always leads to the desired result. Bitsing will predict that you will get a desired result by undertaking a particular activity.

So you know you're going to achieve your goal. When a Bitsing prediction shows that the result will be undesirable, the method will tell you what you need to do to optimise the situation and still book the required result. So success and satisfaction are guaranteed!

I will shortly explain how to predict the results of programmes before rolling them out. It seems an impossible task, but it is not. I will prove that it's possible. And simple. I've used the Bitsing method to successfully predict the achievement of goals that were previously considered impossible to achieve. Yet they were all achieved.

An organisation which had failed to perform as predicted did not fail because of the prediction. People simply did not do what Bitsing prescribed. If the prediction says go left, you should not go to the right. Follow the directions of the Bitsing method closely. Do not fall back into old ways!

Sometimes the results are even better than predicted. Up to three times as much as the objective! Tripled turnover is not as strange a result as it seems. Imagine that you tripled your turnover target. It's impossible you say? Believe me, it can happen.

I am working together with some universities to scientifically explore the causes of this 'over-performance'. It may be that the Bitsing method so perfectly optimises the organisation that everything it does delivers the absolute maximum result, which could be a multiple of that originally targeted. See foreword for information on the current state of affairs in this regard.

If someone claims that nothing can be guaranteed, he just doesn't know how to do it

If you know in advance what your programmes will bring you, you can start them with confidence and launch them to your target groups. Prediction of programme results is an essential part of the Bitsing method. As mentioned, prediction confirms that a programme will produce the necessary results. If not, you can adjust the programme in time and optimise it, so that the required results are still achieved. I will now explain how to predict results. Use these predictions to guide yourself in rolling out the six BITSER programmes. It is a quantified process - when making a prediction, you of course base it on actual figures. On completion of this step you will know that your continuity turnover goal will be achieved.

Two components are needed in order to make the prediction: one in percentages and one in absolute numbers. The percentage component provides insight into your current, achieved success, per BITSER step. The absolute component is the number of customers you need to achieve your turnover target.

Your current success, per BITSER step

If you look at your business or organisation from the point of view of the six BITSER steps you will realise that you do not start this process empty-handed. You already have, of course, a certain amount of awareness, an image, point-of-sale traffic and sales. You will also have extra sales and referral sales. Even if the referred sales are at the level of 0.001% some, no doubt, will have been made.

I call this percentage expression of your current success the 'success ratio'. It shows how successful your current mode of operation is - per BITSER step.

The first thing to be done is to note your current success ratio next to each of the BITSER steps. How many people in your target market have heard of your brand or organisation? Note this percentage next to BITSER step B.

Continue to note the success ratios next to each of the steps. To express your current success in percentages, ask yourself the following questions.

The first is about the decision-makers in your target market, the people who decide whether or not you will achieve your turnover. Assume a broad target group. Not only your existing customers, but all decision makers in the total target group.

THE SUCCESS RATIO OF THE B STEP
What percentage of all decision makers know your brand or organisation's name? Note the answer next to step B.

THE SUCCESS RATIO OF THE I STEP
The next question relates to those standing on the B step.
What percentage of people who know your name are considering your brand, want it, and put it on their list of options? Note the answer next to step I.

THE SUCCESS RATIO OF THE T STEP
The next question relates to those standing on the I step.
What percentage of the people who consider your brand take action - for example visit the store or attend a meeting? Note the answer next to step T.

THE SUCCESS RATIO OF THE S STEP

What percentage of the people who take action proceed to purchase, become a customer?
Note the answer next to step S.

THE SUCCESS RATIO OF THE E STEP

What percentage of people who have bought once remain customers and buy again? Note the answer next to the E step. (This is called the retention percentage.)

THE SUCCESS RATIO OF THE R STEP

What percentage of people who remain customers and continue to buy recruit new customers when requested?
Note the answer next to the R step.

When in doubt about a percentage research it among the target group. Nine out of ten organisations already have the information they need - perhaps concealed somewhere in a department. In any event - the needed information is to be found.

Your end result might look like this:

BITSER STEP	SUCCESS RATIO
B	54%
I	32%
T	40%
S	24%
E	60%
R	4%

What do the success ratios tell you?
The percentages indicate the current situation on each of the BITSER steps: how well the current activities of the organisation perform, measured in terms of results.

But they also tell you something extremely unusual. Something with significant positive impact on your turnover goal.
The success ratios enable you to calculate the total turnover 'potential' of a target group, as a result of your current activities. Select 100 decision makers from your target group and serially apply the success rates to this selection. You will then have predicted what you can expect from your current sales activities. For example:

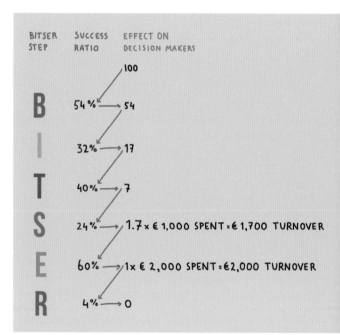

BITSER STEP	SUCCESS RATIO	EFFECT ON DECISION MAKERS
B	54%	100 → 54
I	32%	17
T	40%	7
S	24%	1.7 x € 1,000 SPENT = € 1,700 TURNOVER
E	60%	1 x € 2,000 SPENT = € 2,000 TURNOVER
R	4%	0

So 100 decision-makers currently produce a turnover of € 3,700. If the company today approached 100 decision-makers in the target group, using six BITSER activities, this is the turnover that would result. The percentages and related turnover amounts in effect show how effective the company is in helping people climb the steps of the BITSER stair. They reflect the organisation's current effectiveness.

Apply the right programmes to the right BITSER steps and you can calculate the turnover growth resulting from the improved success percentages. What would happen if the company in the example above improved its effectiveness with the help of appropriate BITSER programmes and thereby increased the success ratios? Awareness, for example, would increase, more people would consider the brand, more traffic would result and more people would buy - and so on. Suppose that the success percentage of the I step, as a result of proper implementation of the programme, grows from 32% to 49%. Turnover will then increase from € 3,700 to € 5,580. Optimising the I step results in an additional € 1,880 turnover - a growth rate of 51%. Increased effectiveness through optimisation has enormous consequences in terms of potential additional turnover.

This should make you want to start immediately. So let's complete the process of predicting your results.

The number of customers needed
An important part of the prediction is the number of customers you will need to ensure the achievement of your turnover objective. Some of these customers will have to be newly recruited (i.e. the number of new customers), others will come from the group of existing customers (i.e. the number of customers to be retained). In a large organisation the required number of customers could run into millions. If your company is small, only a few may be required. Whether your organisation is large or small, the number of customers is critical to your turnover. The term 'customer' is generally understood to mean the person who buys your product. This does not always have to be a physical product. A service is also a product. And so is a behaviour change - for instance getting people to be more energy efficient. You want them to 'buy' (into) the necessary behaviour changes. A customer is therefore someone who does what you want him to do; someone who buys what you offer.

Have you ever stopped to think how many customers you need? Take a guess. And note the number, even if you already know it. I'll demonstrate that your number is incorrect - which in turn would make it difficult to achieve your turnover target. The issue is: How many customers do you really need in order to achieve your turnover goal? Properly determined, this number is your "volume strategy'.

A simple but very valuable calculation
The actual, required number of customers is easily calculated. Three elements are required: your turnover target, the average amount spent and a formula.

You already know your turnover goal. In order to calculate the required number of customers to reach this goal you need to know the amount spent by an average single, unique customer. Identify the amount that an average existing customer spent during a period similar to the period in which you want to achieve your turnover goal. If that period is a year, look at the total amount spent by an average, single customer in a year. Ask yourself: 'What is the total amount spent by an average customer during a year?' This is the actual amount spent. Not what you wish it could be, but what it is.

If a customer on average spends 10 euros per visit and visits seven times a year, then the total average amount spent by the customer is 70 euros. In statistical terms you are calculating the median amount. The average, most frequently occurring, amount spent.

The formula for calculation of the required number of customers is simple: you divide the turnover target by the average amount spent:

$$\text{REQUIRED NUMBER OF CUSTOMERS} = \frac{\text{TURNOVER TARGET}}{\text{AVERAGE AMOUNT SPENT PER CUSTOMER}}$$

You now know how many customers you will need in total during the period in which you must achieve your turnover goal. You already have a turnover goal. Now you also have a commercial goal: obtain the required number of customers.

Once you've applied this calculation and arrived at an indication of the number of customers you need, go back and compare this with the number you first thought was required. As I predicted - you originally under-estimated this number.

What do you do if the amount spent changes?
It is 100% certain that the average amount spent by your customers will change during the months in which you are busy achieving your turnover goal. If it appears that the average customer spend changes, due to circumstances, you must redo the calculation and then focus on acquiring the revised number of customers needed. Check it periodically.

Phasing the required number of customers over time
A continuity turnover goal is not achieved in one fell swoop. This takes time, namely the period you set for achieving that goal. Achievement of the turnover goal will therefore be spread over time. In practice, large organisations divide the period of achievement of their turnover goal into quarters, over which the amount of the revenue goal is spread. Medium sized organisations use months and small ones weeks. The required number of customers is then calculated per period and converted into a BITSER results prediction.

This gives a complete overview of what must happen in each period. Bitsing makes things very specific. And the more tangible something is, the easier it is to understand and apply.

Perfecting results prediction
You have now predicted the number of customers required in order to achieve your turnover goal. Using this fact you now proceed step by step to complete the BITSER prediction. This process is not complicated.

Always start with the predicted results of the SER steps
Two types of customers make up the required number of customers. There is the number of existing customers, which you must retain. These are on the E step. And there is the number of new clients, located on the S and R steps. Existing and new customers together constitute the required number of customers.

Schematic example of an SER results prediction:

BITSER PROGRAMME	NUMBER	SUCCES RATIO	PREDICTION
S PROGRAMME			213
E PROGRAMME	300	60%	180
R PROGRAMME	180	4%	7

If you know how many existing customers are in your current portfolio, for instance 300, and then apply the E step success ratio percentage to this number, for instance 60%, you will have predicted how many customers are retained, namely 180. This number is noted against the E step. And this is your completed results prediction for the E step. Continue the results prediction process by first calculating the number of new customers required for the R step. The outcome in the example is 7.
If, as per the example, 400 customers are required to achieve the continuity goal, and you subtract the customers on the E and R steps from this number, the balance of customers to be recruited is 213. This number is entered on the S step,

with the outcome being the (very significant) total number of clients required.

The success ratio of the R step represents a percentage. In the example given it is 4%. That means that 4% of the retained customers (there are 180 in the example) will successfully acquire new customers for you. 4% (the R percentage) of this number is 7 new customers (to be recruited by retained customers). These will be referral sales, so they are placed on the R step.

This concludes the prediction of results for the S, E and R programmes. Together these numbers guarantee achievement of the turnover goal.

Proceed with the predicted results of the BIT steps
It is now easy to compete the results forecast: predict the outcomes of the remaining three programmes (the BIT programmes) using the relevant success ratios.

Schematic example of a BIT results prediction:

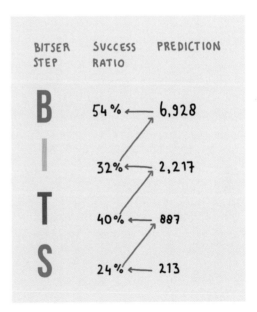

BITSER STEP	SUCCESS RATIO	PREDICTION
B	54% ←	6,928
I	32% ←	2,217
T	40% ←	887
S	24% ←	213

The result of the S step is required for prediction of the T-step. Take the predicted number for the S step as starting point. In the example this is 213. The T step prediction is made using the S step's success ratio, 24%. The S step requires 213 new customers. This number is therefore represented by 24%. The number on the T step is therefore 100/24 x 213 = 887. And this is the specific, guaranteed result of the T programme.

This process is repeated for the remaining steps. The end result will be the predicted results of each of the BITSER programmes. As these are fact-based predictions, you can trust that they will be achieved. You have laid the foundation for obtaining successful results from all six of the BITSER programmes. Your turnover goal is within reach! Your undoubtedly excellent BITSER programmes will affect these success ratios and therefore also your predicted results. I will explain later how to deal with that situation.

From prediction to target group reach
To achieve goals you need to reach people. You need them, after all, in order to achieve your turnover goal. Reaching people in the target group makes the difference between success and failure.

If you approach too few people you will have correspondingly lower results and less turnover. In order to achieve your turnover goal each BITSER programme must approach the required number of people. I call this number the 'required programme reach'. Your route to success starts with knowing the numbers of people which each of the programmes has to reach, i.e. the number of people, per step, who must be addressed by the programme for that step. If a programme does not reach this required number of people, the predicted outcome will also not be achieved.

If programmes are able to reach the number of target group members required in order to achieve a particular result, then that result is guaranteed. Determination of programme reach is therefore a critical part of the prediction process. This requires an additional, small step. The defined programme reach is the same as the predicted outcome of the previous programme. The result of programme B is, of course, the reach of the I programme. And the result of the I programme, in turn, is the reach of the T programme.

BITSER PROGRAMME	REACH	SUCCESS RATIO	PREDICTION
B PROGRAMME	12,829	← 54%	← 6,928
I PROGRAMME	6,928	← 32%	← 2,217
T PROGRAMME	2,217	← 40%	← 887
S PROGRAMME	887	← 24%	← 213

NOTE: THE NUMBER OF PEOPLE TO BE APPROACHED VIA THE E-PROGRAMME IS A SPECIAL CASE. THE PEOPLE TO BE REACHED ON THE E-STEP ARE ALL EXISTING CUSTOMERS.

E PROGRAMME	300	→ 60%	→ 180
R PROGRAMME	180	→ 4%	→ 7

Please refer to the earlier chart, showing examples of results prediction, in order to see how the results of the BITSER steps reveal the programme reach numbers. These numbers predict how many people need to be reached, per step, in order to ensure that the predicted outcome will be achieved. I call this the 'winning reach', as it is the number that ensures that you win.

You can formulate a prediction for each target group with which you are dealing and for any period in which you want to achieve turnover targets - for example for a year, a quarter, a month or even for a week. In any situation in which you're approaching markets and target groups, the results of the programmes you are going to roll out should be predicted. The process of prediction of reach and result is now complete. Although... there is still a snag.

What if there are not enough people in my target group?

Imagine that you need to approach a target group in which the required number of people is simply not present. The number of people to be reached is greater than the market volume. If there are not enough people to climb the steps of the BITSER stair, the goals will not be achieved.

I experienced a situation in which a railway company had to approach 60 million consumers in order to achieve its turnover target. This number of people was just not available. At most, 33 million were. In this situation you can roll out programmes until you are blue in the face - your turnover goal will still not be met. Yet the railway company succeeded! What do you do when your target group does not supply enough people? Read on.

Optimise!

If the number of people you are required to reach are not in your target group you have a red flag situation. There are too few people available to achieve your objectives. In which case it makes no sense to apply the BITSER programmes. Something has to happen first to make that feasible. You can check if there is a red flag situation, by comparing the total number of available people in your target group (excluding your own customers) to the number of people that have to be reached according to the results prediction: i.e. compare the number in target group to the number to be reached. The latter number can be found on the B step. In the example on the left it is 12,829.

The challenge is to decrease the reach of the B programme to equal the number of available people in the target group. If this can be achieved you can look forward to a successful result. The predicted reach of a B programme must be at least as large as the number of available persons in the target group. A red flag situation arises because one or more of the BITSER step success ratios is or are too low. Therefore many more people have to be reached than are present in the target group. The higher a success ratio, the lower the number of people that have to be reached. A red flag situation can thus be solved by improving success ratios. This is, of course, achieved by using BITSER programmes. But not all six. Only use the programmes the success ratios of which are the cause of the red flag. These are the worst-scoring ratios - the top three in your BITSER ranking (see law 4).

So the 'problem' ratios must first be optimised. Then a complete BITSER programme must be implemented. Optimising success ratios requires additional, interim investment - which, again, is not simply a process of throwing money at all six programmes. Select only the poorly performing ratios.

After optimisation you will immediately see that your prediction looks more optimistic. If a red flag situation arises, the only thing you have to do is optimise the low-scoring ratios - and keep on doing so until the required reach of the B programme equates to the number of people in the target group. The railway company mentioned earlier managed, by optimising poor success ratios, to reduce its required target group reach to 18 million people. A number sufficient to enable them to achieve their goal.

The prediction is complete. Now you know how the Bitsing method guarantees results.

Checking a BITSER ranking

In law 4 you read all about the BITSER ranking. This ranking shows the relative importance of an obstacle on any given step of the BITSER stair. As you will recall, the BITSER ranking indicates how to set your priorities and results in your ideal plan of action. You can test this ranking. In fact, the success ratios do this for you. The lower a success ratio, the higher a BITSER step ranked position. Starting from the beginning of the BITSER stair the lower success ratio is given a higher priority ranking.

Compare the two rankings alongside the success ratios. Which of the two is correct?

BITSER LEVEL	SUCCESS RATIOS	RANKING 1	RANKING 2
B	64%	5	4
I	32%	1	3
T	40%	4	6
S	24%	2	1
E	60%	6	5
R	4%	3	2

THE ANSWER IS RANKING 1. THE REASONING IS 'TOP TO BOTTOM', AS THE BIGGER VOLUME OF TARGET GROUP PEOPLE ARE AT THE BEGINNING OF THE BITSER STAIR. WHEN A LOW SUCCES RATIO IS LOCATED AT THE BEGINNING OF THE BITSER STAIR RECEIVES HIGHER PRIORITY.

What if the facts change?

If the percentages of the success ratios change, the prediction changes with them. You may, for instance, be successful in implementing the BITSER programmes, thereby improving the success ratios. If so, the results prediction changes as well - and, indeed, positively. The higher the ratios, the fewer people you need to reach to accomplish your goals. Improved ratios result in cost efficiency: you have to reach fewer people, which costs less money. However, it can also happen that the success ratios worsen. It may rain heavily, reducing store visits. The T step ratio will then decrease. Don't worry - the predicted numbers will automatically change. This means, at most, that you'll have to reach more people to arrive at the required number of customers. The process can never go wrong.

Results prediction affects how your organisation is structured

A prediction is an essential element in structuring your organisation. Knowing the reach and results of each BITSER programme enables you to prepare the organisation well for what is to come. Include everyone involved in goal-achievement in the prediction - yourself, your colleagues and all relevant parties. After all, if people don't know what needs to

be achieved in a given period, they won't achieve it. For instance, if you don't know how much turnover has to be earned today, or which programme has to reach which number of people, that targeted amount will not be earned.

The prediction indicates how many people in the audience should be approached within a period and, accordingly, what the expected result will be. It shows how many visitors can be expected in a period, and how many customers will result from that. All of this has consequences for how the organisation is structured.

The marketing team will benefit from the clear understanding of the requirements for (development of) support for this process. This facilitates drawing up the programme's associated media plans. The sales team will know how many people in the target group will react. So it will know how many people need to be approached in order to recruit them as customers. It will also know the predicted sales results of this activity. The after-sales department will know how many existing customers they have to approach, in order to achieve the predicted extra sales. In fact, every employee in your organisation will be ready to perform his

or her role in dealing with predicted results.

Create a BITSER programme calendar

Create a BITSER programme calendar for each sub-period. You will find, in practice, that the calendar for each, subsequent sub-period will be subject to change - as a result of actual changes in the facts on which it is based. Note the turnover target for the period, as well as the required programme reach and the predicted result. At the end of the period you will measure whether they have been achieved. These results will, in turn, influence your update of calendar activities for the next period.

Take into account the time between the start of the B programme and the moment of achieving the required turnover. It will come as no surprise that you will be implementing programmes to reach the turnover of a particular period while at the same time preparing the programmes that drive achievement of turnover in later periods.

BITSER PROGRAMME MANAGEMENT KALENDAR

PROGRAMME		KEY AUDIENCE	# REACH	FREQUENCY	RESPONSIBLE	PERIOD											
						1	2	3	4	5	6	7	8	9	10	11	12
B	MEDIUM 1																
	MEDIUM 2																
	MEDIUM 3																
I	MEDIUM 1																
	MEDIUM 2																
	MEDIUM 3																
T	MEDIUM 1																
	MEDIUM 2																
	MEDIUM 3																
S	MEDIUM 1																
	MEDIUM 2																
	MEDIUM 3																
E	MEDIUM 1																
	MEDIUM 2																
	MEDIUM 3																
R	MEDIUM 1																
	MEDIUM 2																
	MEDIUM 3																

LAW 7

ENSURE PROFIT AND AVOID FINANCIAL DISASTERS

NEVER SPEND MORE MONEY THAN A PROGRAMME CAN EARN

Have you ever paid for something that you weren't sure of getting? The chances of this are small. It would be rather strange if you asked for bread at the bakery, paid for it and then had to leave without the bread. Yet this happens every day, in almost every organisation. Millions are spent on things about which no one has any idea of what, if anything, they will deliver. This will not be the case here. Even 10 euros is too much to spend if you get nothing in return. And the main cause of wasted money? People don't invest in a goal. The process and need for determining goals has been dealt with at length under law 1. Including the observation that not everything one thinks of as a goal, is actually a goal. I noted that

an organisation's strategy or its employees' tasks are often elevated to the status of goals - and that this then obscures the reason for the strategy or task's existence in the first place. This 'reason' is the real goal - the strategy and task merely help you achieve it. It is a fact that organisations tend to invest in their strategy and employee tasks, but forget that they are making this investment in order to achieve a goal. They do not invest in the goal - which is in fact then forgotten - but in the path that leads to it. Which places a question mark above achievement of the real goal. In this situation the chance of a negative result is high. The rule is that your goal must be the main focus of your investment.

You already know your real goal: the achievement of your continuity turnover target. This goal and this goal only is the reason that the organisation exists. Making your turnover goal central makes the process of investing to achieve it much easier, more effective and, most importantly, more efficient.

Now try making your turnover goal central. Just write the amount on a piece of paper, if you haven't already done so after reading law 1. Now look at what you are investing to achieve it. You will conclude that these investments gives you no certainty of financial return. Would you invest a million if you knew in advance that your return will only be half of that amount? Of course not. Would you invest the same million if you knew that you would double it? Of course! This what it's all about. Everything you do should produce more money than it cost you - or at least the same as the amount invested if profit is not the objective. If you invest more than it yields, you make a loss. If you invest less, you make a profit and have extra cash at hand.

Do not invest more money than your programmes can produce

When helping organisations implement the Bitsing method, I am often amazed at how many of them haphazardly make budgets available for activities of unknown profitability or loss potential. Their attitude is that 'the risk is part of the cost' - and so they continue blindly to invest. Use the Bitsing method - and this will not happen. Money will only be spent if it is certain that the activity will generate more money than it cost. We are going to guarantee profit. (Note: this is sometimes called ROI, but I will show that the entire concept of ROI is nonsense.)

What ROI really means

The term ROI is commonly taken to mean 'return on investment'. ROI stands for what you get back from an investment.

But what is that exactly? What do you actually get back as return on your investment? According to this definition, it could be anything. The traditional business definition of ROI is much too broad, too superficial, has no deeper meaning. This book has already made amply clear that the Bitsing method represents the new modern economic era. It's an approach in which tools and terms are specifically defined - so there's no room for the 'free translation' of meaning that ROI invites. Accordingly, in the world of Bitsing, the term and concept of ROI - return on investment - just don't exist.

What if your 'return' is a financial loss and collapses your organisation? You can achieve a great 'return' on your investment with increased sales and new customers - but you can still go bankrupt because you paid too much for the return.

So from now on we'll only talk about ROS. With the Bitsing method you can now look forward to having a Remainder On Spend - in which you end up with more money than you spent on achieving your objectives (a Remain). Traditional business thinking was happy with 'return on investment'. In Bitsing we focus on the positive financial remain, delivered by the money you spent -

the Remainder On Spend. This is what it's all about. And, as you can see, I'd also rather not talk about 'investment' at all, but rather about 'spending'. Investment implies that you never know what you will get in return. While with expenditure you know precisely. For this reason people never ask, 'How much did you invest at the supermarket today?' What they do ask is, "How much did you spend in the supermarket today?' Forget ROI, say hello to ROS: Remainder On Spend.

Preventing financial disasters

"We focus on ROI," I hear all too often. If I question this statement, it turns out that they do post-evaluation on whether activities yielded a return or not. Indeed, everything can be evaluated in retrospect, but if you really want to achieve financial success you should already know in advance whether an activity is going to deliver ROS, a remain.

How do you ensure that your BITSER programmes will bring in more money than they cost, so you always have money in your bank account? If you know how to do this, you are assured of a Remainder On Spend (ROS). So when I write about about yield or result, I mean ROS.

It is imperative to ensure that the yield (ROS) of all programmes is expressed and known. This avoids the financial failures that result, for instance, from making budgets available in a haphazard manner without knowing what they will yield. Expenditure is only justified when it's based on ROS.

Predicting yield (ROS)

It is possible to predict the yield of BITSER programmes. To guarantee that yield you have to know what you'll get in return for your expenditure - in advance. How is this done? The concepts involved are simple and the process and its context are easy to understand. My explanation relies on an example in which a company with a turnover goal of €175,000,000 derives a profit of €17,500,000 (10%).
Let's work through the practical rules for predicting and guaranteeing your ROS.

Perform the following analyses:

1 CALCULATE PROFIT
2 DETERMINE THE BITSER EXPENDITURE CEILING
3 QUANTIFY THE BITSER EXPENDITURE PLAN
4 PREDICT YIELD (ROS)

ANALYSIS 1 PROFIT

Profit is the positive difference between turnover and cost (the costs of operating the organisation as a whole, including of course the costs of implementing its BITSER programmes). Profit is related to the turnover target of your Bitsing plan. In this sense: what profit do you make on the turnover goal in the Bitsing plan? Calculate the profit you want to make over the entire, targeted period, for instance the annual profit.

If you have no profit objective, use the amount that will cover your expense as equivalent to profit. Take cost increases into account - prices have a tendency to rise.

ANALYSIS 2
THE BITSER EXPENDITURE CEILING

'Expenditure Ceiling' is a useful concept. It is the maximum amount that may be spent on a programme without making a loss. This maximum spend is also the so-called break-even spend. Expenditure may not exceed this amount.

The cost of implementing the Bitsing plan and, specifically, the BITSER programmes should never exceed the profit, otherwise the programmes will make a loss.

The company profit therefore equates to the amount of the expenditure ceiling. After all, if you spend more than the profit, you will get a loss in return. The expenditure ceiling helps to rein in the organisation's expenditure, ensuring that it remains financially sound and justified. The expenditure ceiling must never be exceeded. In fact in most cases you must remain safely below it. Otherwise there will be no Remain On Spend (ROS). The profit target is the sum of the amounts of the total expenditure ceilings of all programmes. You can now calculate the expenditure ceiling of the individual programmes; later this will be used to determine ROS per programme.

An expenditure ceiling per BITSER programme

The programme strategy focus percentages (see law 5) represent the shares of each programme in the expenditure ceiling. Applying these percentages to the total amount of the expenditure ceiling instantly gives you the amount you can spend on the development and implementation of each BITSER programme while breaking even on that amount. You can also immediately see the amount of profit you will forgo if you fail to deploy one or more of the BITSER programmes. If programme expenditure remains below the ceiling they will deliver more than they cost and you have a yield (ROS).

Example of an Expenditure ceiling overview:

BITSER PROGRAMME	STRATEGY*	CEILING*
B PROGRAMME	15%	€ 2,500,000
I PROGRAMME	30%	€ 5,000,000
T PROGRAMME	20%	€ 3,300,000
S PROGRAMME	25%	€ 4,150,000
E PROGRAMME	10%	€ 1,700,000
R PROGRAMME	5%	€ 850,000
	105%	€ 17,500,000

* THE FOCUS PERCENTAGES ARE ROUNDED (SEE LAW 5). THE TOTAL OF ALL PERCENTAGES IS 105%. THE AMOUNTS UNDER 'CEILING' ARE BASED ON UNROUNDED PERCENTAGES.

ANALYSIS 3
THE BITSER EXPENDITURE PLAN

I cannot tell you here what absolute amount of expenditure you need in order to achieve your turnover goal. I know too little of your situation. I also don't have your Bitsing plan in front of me. On the other hand, you do know what resources you need and what they will cost - at least, if you have drawn up a Bitsing plan. However, I can show you how to guarantee your ROS.

The expenditures are the amounts needed to develop, produce and roll out the programmes with which you are going to achieve your turnover target. You may limit this to the cost of the actual programmes, but you may also include the cost of the personnel required to implement the programmes (for example, the cost of a marketing and sales team).

You can go as far as you think necessary, as long as the costs are in service of the programmes rolled out to achieve your turnover goal. Leasing new machinery falls outside the scope of a BITSER expenditure plan, as it will not directly increase your turnover. This cost should be already included in the profit calculation (see analysis 1). The resources, on the other hand, as described in law 5, are indeed components of the BITSER spending plan. Expenditure plans must be compiled for each BITSER programme. Total expenditure is the amount needed to achieve the continuity turnover goal with the six BITSER programmes. Always ensure that programme expenditure is in line with programme strategy. For example, if a programme has a focus share of 5% of the total palette of programmes, spending cannot be a multiple of that percentage.

ANALYSIS 4 PREDICTING REMAINDER ON SPEND (ROS)

The above analyses have made the terms 'expenditure ceiling' and 'expenditure plan' clear. The amount of the expenditure ceiling is the maximum amount that you can spend on a programme without making either a yield or a loss. However, what you naturally want is a guaranteed, positive result. The expenditure plan amount comes into play here. The difference between the expenditure ceiling and expenditure spending plan amounts is the yield, the remainder (ROS).

If all BITSER programme ROS predictions are positive, the amount of expenditure will be significantly lower than the ceiling and you can roll out the programmes with confidence.

If a programme's ROS prediction is negative you should critically review the expenditures in that programme. Programme expenditure in excess of the expenditure ceiling can and do, of course, happen.

applied the model to all of its data streams. A very demanding process, but also a very rewarding one: their turnover almost tripled.

BITSER PROGRAMME	STRATEGY*	CEILING*	EXPENDITURE	ROS
B PROGRAMME	15%	€ 2,500,000	€ 290,000	€ 2,210,000
I PROGRAMME	30%	€ 5,000,000	€ 580,000	€ 4,420,000
T PROGRAMME	20%	€ 3,300,000	€ 385,000	€ 2,915,000
S PROGRAMME	25%	€ 4,150,000	€ 490,000	€ 3,660,000
E PROGRAMME	10%	€ 1,700,000	€ 170,000	€ 1,530,000
R PROGRAMME	5%	€ 850,000	€ 85,000	€ 765,000
	105%	€ 17,500,000	€ 2,000,000	€ 15,500,000

* THE FOCUS PERCENTAGES ARE ROUNDED (SEE LAW 5). THE TOTAL OF ALL PERCENTAGES IS 105%. THE AMOUNTS UNDER 'CEILING' ARE BASED ON UNROUNDED PERCENTAGES.

I have tried to keep this explanation of the ROS principle as simple as possible. In practice, the model has been applied in the most complex situations. Hewlett Packard Enterprice EMEA, for example,

ANALYSES FOR PREDICTING YIELD

1 CALCULATE PROFIT
2 DETERMINE THE BITSER
   EXPENDITURE CEILING
3 QUANTIFY THE BITSER
   EXPENDITURE PLAN
4 PREDICT YIELD (ROS)

How do you handle unexpected expenditure?

It can happen that you have to deal with unexpected costs. An unpleasant task. In foreseeable situations one is able to postpone additional expenses, or simply not incur them, but unexpected expenditure can be unavoidable. Always therefore monitor actual programme expenditure in relation to Remain On Spend (ROS) and the expenditure ceiling. If you stay within positive ROS, additional costs will not negatively impact your profit. However, if extra costs exceed the expenditure ceiling, losses will be incurred. These touchstones enable you to quickly decide whether unforeseen additional expenditure will or will not be incurred.

BITSER PROGRAMME SHARE OF TURNOVER

Each of the BITSER programmes are responsible for part of the turnover to be achieved. Omit a programme and you run the risk of losing a substantial slice of your turnover. The programme strategy helps you calculate programme share. The chart below presents an example. The business has a turnover goal of 250.000.000 euros.

	BITSER PROGRAMME	FOCUS STRATEGY	SHARE OF TURNOVER *
B	PROGRAMME	20%	€ 50,000,000
I	PROGRAMME	30%	€ 75,000,000
T	PROGRAMME	25%	€ 62,500,000
S	PROGRAMME	10 %	€ 25,000,000
E	PROGRAMME	5%	€ 12,500,000
R	PROGRAMME	15%	€ 37,500,000

* TOTAL TURNOVER EXEEDS TURNOVER GOAL BY 5% DUE TO ROUNDING.

Scrapping the I programme would expose the business to the risk of losing 75.000.000 in turnover. If the business were to focus exclusively on sales and only use the S programme, it would only be certain of making a turnover of 25,000,000 euros, i.e. 17% of the goal.

IGNORANCE IS FAR FROM BLISS

Measurement is vital!

I'm tempted to say that measurement is the most important aspect of the Bitsing method, were it not that the other aspects are equally important. It is, however, vital. Without measurement you can't operate on the basis of facts - and factual information is the backbone of this methodology. Circumstances change - and the answers provided by the Bitsing method change with them. I try to have a healthy lifestyle, without denying myself anything. I believe in enjoying life, experiencing it to the full. But in a way that allows me to live as long as possible - otherwise there won't be time to do what I still want to do. So it's a question of balancing pleasure and health, one might say. There are times when it is hard to find that balance, when pleasure takes the upper hand. And there are times I look at the scale - which never fails to tell me when it's time for a little lifestyle adjustment. So I adjust. I exercise more, eat healthier, get more sleep.

Organisations also have lives. They should also do everything they can to live as long as possible, without denying themselves some pleasure. An organisation will therefore also have to regularly bring itself back into balance, in order to remain healthy and keep its employees happy.

We weigh ourselves, so why don't organisations check how they measure up? If you do not know that there is something wrong, you can do nothing to fix it. Ignorance is far from bliss.

So measure!

Evaluating your programmes' results equips you to enter the next phase. However, the aspects that affect your choices change. All the issues I described in seven laws will change over time. Which means you have to change your reaction to them, by updating your Bitsing plan. This is the only way you can ensure that future turnover targets will continue to be achieved, with yield. What would happen if a new product or service becomes dominant in terms of its share of your turnover? It will have to become the new topic in your purchasing behaviour programmes. What if the average customer order amount changes? It will influence the number of customers you need to recruit and retain, therefore, the prediction of your programmes' results. In short, monitoring, measurement, evaluation, learning from experience and adapting are all essential for the continuity of your organisation. Investigate whether the facts on which your Bitsing plan is based have changed, draw lessons from this and make the necessary

adjustments. The contents of this book are your best guide to what has to be measured and how.

CHECKLIST AND SELF-HELP TOOLS

SUMMARY

1. HAVE YOU FORMULATED A CONTINUITY GOAL AS TARGET?

2. WHEN MAKING CHOICHES DO YOU FOCUS ON HARD, FINANCIAL FACTS?

3. IS YOUR APPROACH TO THE MARKET UNBEATABLE?

4. DO YOUR PLANS GET THE MOST OUT OF EVERY PERSON IN YOUR TARGET GROUPS?

5. DO YOU ACHIEVE THIS BY USING ONLY EFFECTIVE PROGRAMMES

6. DO YOU PREDICT RESULTS BEFORE ROLL-OUT?

7. DO YOU SPEND LESS MONEY ON PROGRAMME ACTIVITIES THAN THEY ARE CAPABLE OF PRODUCING?

PER LAW

LAW 1 ALWAYS SET A CONTINUITY GOAL
- First formulate the turnover goal crucial for the continuity of your organisation in its current form.
- Formulate two extra turnover targets, the ambition goal and the dream goal.

LAW 2 ENSURE THAT YOU ACHIEVE YOUR GOAL
- Communicate, because without communication, nothing happens and you do not reach your goal. Don't do nothing. Take action.
- Making decisions focus on hard financial facts and not on assumptions. You can only gamble on assumptions.
- Never act haphazardly. When building a house you don't start with the walls. Provide a good strategic foundation that takes you in the right direction.
- Make the right choices. Apply the pencils philosophy. It will make you successful.
- Structure your organisation in line with the pencils focus strategy percentages.

LAW 3 BE UNBEATABLE
- Overcome the obstacles, not your problems! These are the obstacles

within your target group, which obstruct achievement of your turnover goal. They are no less - but also no more - than that.

- Someone must 'want' you before they 'buy' you and 'remain' as a customer. BITSER ranking enables you to develop a focus strategy which, in one stroke and with the correct degree of focus, will build preference for your brand, buying behaviour for your products or services and loyalty for your organisation and its other products and services - both free and paid for.

- Develop a policy which comprises: a preference policy for your brand, driven by the brand's role in society and including its emotional propositions; a purchasing behaviour policy - about your product/service, the promise that it delivers and its rational propositions; a loyalty policy that asserts the added value of your internal organisation, as well as the relational propositions.

- The proposition contained in a policy is what you offer, the relevant benefit. It has a prominent voice in your activities. Ascertain whether it should be an emotional, rational or relational proposition. You will know which propositions you may and, in particular, may not use, as a result of carrying out

a scorecard analysis.

- The scorecard analysis will also enable you to identify your own 'golden egg'. Your 'most relevant' characteristic - the thing that makes you uncopyable. This is expressed in the factual description of your uncopyability factor.

- Your golden egg gives all of your propositions credibility in the eyes of your target groups. It also guides you in the activities you undertake with regard to your markets and target groups.

LAW 4 MAKE THE MOST OF EVERY PERSON IN YOUR TARGET GROUP

- Help everyone in your target group climb the steps of the BITSER stair.

- Always first compile a BITSER ranking, to expose the obstacles in the target group.

- Use the BITSER ranking to translate the obstacle analysis into an action plan.

- Ensure that you roll out six BITSER programmes.

- Teach yourself and your organisation not to think in target groups, but in target person profiles. There are seven: Suspects, Potentials, Preferrers, Movers, Buyers, Users, Sellers. This facilitates communication when it comes to implementing the programmes.

LAW 5 ONLY DEPLOY EFFECTIVE PROCESSES AND PROGRAMMES

- The BITSER programme strategy ensures that the correct degree of emphasis is placed on each of the internal and external activities of your organisation.

- Structure and resource your organisation on the basis of the requirements of the programme strategy and the BITSER techniques.

- A BITSER programme has a task, subject and proposition and is founded on its own technical criteria.

- Resources and media are not all the same. Base your selection on what the programme strategy requires. There are six types of resources and media: teasing, positioning, activating, convincing, satisfying and relational. Your programme strategy shows, at a glance, which should be dominant, less dominant or avoided.

- A BITSER programme brings together multiple activities, performed in a given period. The intensity and the duration of a programme are determined by the programme strategy. Programmes have introductory, building or maintenance strategies.

- Translate your uncopyability factor into a slogan or metaphor, recognisable by everyone involved in the programme activities of the organisation.

LAW 6 PREDICT RESULTS BEFORE ROLLING OUT PROGRAMMES

- A results prediction makes a successful outcome certain. Produce one before you implement a programme activity.
- The basis for creating a results prediction for your programme activities is how your organisation scored on the BITSER steps, today; your current success ratios.
  Start with this information and complete your prediction. Adjust your current and planned activities as required by the prediction.
- The results prediction will tell how many target group people your programme must reach in order to guarantee the predicted result. A resource or medium selected for use in a programme must be capable of reaching the desired number of people.
- Distribute your turnover goal over sub-periods. Create results predictions and a calendar per sub-period and roll out the activities according to the prediction. Mission accomplished!

LAW 7 ENSURE PROFIT AND AVOID FINANCIAL DISASTERS

- Never spend more money on a programme activity than it will earn.

If your results prediction is replenished with financial figures your profit is guaranteed.
- Calculate the expenditure ceiling - the amount you can spend without making a profit or a loss.
  Your programme spend should remain below this ceiling. If you have drawn up an expenditure plan you can calculate the predicted yield from a programme
- known as Remainder On Spend, or ROS. If this is positive, you can be confident of implementing it. If the predicted ROS is negative you must adapt your expenditure plan.
- Measure - so you're certain of your facts. The Bitsing method is largely based on factual information. And, of course, facts are true. Historical information says nothing about what to expect in the near future, and the future itself is an expectation. If you have completed a period of programme activities investigate whether anything has changed. Draw lessons from the changes, adjust your Bitsing plan to the new facts and start the next round of programme activities. Success is assured.

Self-Help: bitsing.com
Especially for readers of this book there is a website which contains numerous advices and tools to help you to create, execute and monitor your own Bitsing plans and to coach you through the implementation of this amazing method: Bitsing.com.

GLOSSERY OF SPECIAL TERMINOLOGY

A number of terms related to Bitsing tend to crop up in daily practice. It is useful to know what they mean.

✱ BITSING

Bitsing is the entire discipline. The field or world of Bitsing. Also indicated by the umbrella term, 'Bitsing method', as used in this book. Organisations in the process of actively applying the Bitsing method in their operations are 'bitsing'.

✱ BITSING METHOD

The Bitsing method comprises three elements: the seven laws or principles to be followed, the models you use and a range of analysis criteria which give substance to Bitsing plans.

✱ BITSER

The person within an organisation responsible for bitsing. A bitser has acquired knowledge through training courses, seminars or other sources. A bitser understands the method-ology, but is not yet an expert in the field (See 'Bitseter').

✱ BITSETER

A person trained in the art of Bitsing. A Bitseter can professionally apply the methodology and generate Bitsing plans and advice. A Bitseter often has a recognised tertiary degree which includes a Bitsing component.

✱ BITS

To bits an organisation's plans or decisions is to test or evaluate them using the Bitsing method. To bits is to check and optimise existing and planned activities, using the Bitsing method. 'We have to bits this programme' means that the programme has to be made to conform to the Bitsing criteria.

✱ BITSED

A process is or has been bitsed once it has successfully fulfilled the requirements of the Bitsing method and has been evaluated and optimised. 'The programme is bitsed' means it has been tested against and complies with the Bitsing requirements.

Bitsing, Bitsing method, Bitser, Bitseter, Bits, Bitsed ... are terms you will increasingly frequently encounter.

INTERVIEW 1 SHELL INTERNATIONAL

SVEN KRAMER

I write many blogs. I do this, on the one hand, to share the benefits of my Bitsing method and on the other hand to inspire people who are on the way to achieving their goals. The blogs are widely read. And one of them drew an unusual response: "Bitsing remains impressive in its simplicity and accuracy".

It came from Sven Kramer, Senior Strategy, Planning & Performance Management Lead at one of the world's biggest companies, Shell.

The positions Sven has occupied during his long career at Shell could fill their own chapter in this book. Rarely have I seen such an impressive career. So I am not surprised that Sven is responsible, at general management level, for 'global business performance management in support of capital investment decisions

worth billions'. And I expect this makes him a source of inspiration when it comes to the business of making difficult decisions. So I am pleased and surprised when the subject of this impressive resume responds to my request for an interview with an immediate 'yes'. More so when he continues, "I have great confidence in your method. In fact, a smart colleague recently applied the theory to show that a large-scale, inter-national initiative was not all that profitable". I was, of course, flattered - and keen to know more. Join me, as I learn a few things from a conversation with Sven Kramer.

We're in the room in which Sven once attended one of my Bitsing Master Classes. "I still remember attending that inspirational master class here", said Sven. "Your method has had some great successes. You will continue to grow, of course, if you just continue to apply your own model", he smiles.

Sven has been inspired by Bitsing, in a number of ways. But what has intrigued him most is the method's ability to detect answers to complex problems using fact-based models. "It's this factual aspect that I find so special. It's what occupies Shell each day; making things ... factual. We don't just take action. Everything is tested, made fact-based, as it were.

Because what we are doing represents investments of billions."

"In my role as international Strategic Advisor", says Sven, "I received a question requiring the full attention of my colleagues and myself - as unprecedentedly large investments are involved, with equally large risks if it all goes wrong. The question concerned a new energy source - one that is hidden deep in the earth. (I'll just use the general term 'new energy source' here, to avoid a long technical explanation.)"

"This new energy source had seen a lot of growth in some parts of the world, and the question was where else we could grow this new energy source? So they engaged my department to find out."

"At the outset you think of the big financial potential; the resource is everywhere. But this quickly narrows to: 'But where, precisely?' So yes, we search, worldwide, at the locations where we think we'll find it. And we went for it. We invested. We searched. But it gradually became apparent that it wasn't going all that well. A kind of awareness dawned: We think we'll find it somewhere ... but how factually correct is that thought, in itself?

"Then you arrived, with the Master class on your Bitsing method. Your approach to making choices, in the form of the pencil philosophy, was particularly relevant to this problem, and we applied the model to our situation with the new energy source."

"The issue is that we work in many different countries, all over the world. And the size of the investments involved and, indeed, of the world as exploration area, are a cause of concern. The investing starts with the first geological analysis, which of course costs money. Then there are the next steps, each of which cost even more money. I'll keep it simple for the reader, but think of drilling a well, or a number of them; the amount of money you invest without knowing what it's going to yield, grows with each step. And if there are, ultimately, cautious, positive signals, you're not there yet. You must then build a whole lot of facilities and pipelines, and invest an even larger amount.
In short, all the stages you pass through and all the investments must at least be repaid. However, you don't know in advance whether those cost will be recovered."

Sven remains quiet for a moment. "Do you know that only a minority of the pilot projects are ultimately successful? Yet the investments in the majority of the unsuccessful attempts,

or where we should have stopped projects earlier, must also be recovered?
This corresponds to those experienced in product innovation in general. Only about one innovation in ten is successful - and that one success must cover the investment in the other nine innovation attempts.

"That means", continues Sven, "That this, single, successful project, that will undergo full development, must pay for all the projects, worldwide, that are not successful. And that is a lot of expense.

If you do the sums you quickly conclude that you need to raise your strike rate. Partly on the basis of your pencils model and the philosophy behind it.

We started costing out all aspects of the new energy source; using numbers which, as your model says, must be based on hard financial facts. This showed that our focus model actually wasn't so great," said Sven, his tone reflecting the negative impact of this discovery.,"The focus on this new energy source was out of proportion - far too big in relation to its expected turnover, to its capacity to produce a positive yield. That yield appeared more marginal than what we can make on traditional oil and gas - in other words from our 'sharp pencils',

to use your terminology", said Sven.

"So the new energy source was a 'blunt pencil', but one that got an amount of attention comparable to that given to our sharpest pencils, namely oil and gas. And we had to use its much smaller margin to cover a very large investment, with a much lower chance of success. So, yes, as often happens with the Bitsing model, we had to conclude that our initial approach didn't look too good from a commercial point of view. The degree of focus, of course, had to change. So we did that. We first looked at making a more intensive version equivalent to your model; at how we could refine the model and adapt it to our complex processes. By applying a more factual focus, based on financial facts, we aimed to increase the success rate of our selections.

We started identifying criteria, which raise the chance of financial success. We called them the Big Rules. If a project didn't suffi-ciently match the criteria, we immediately stopped it. We stopped earlier than before, in this way keeping the costs as low as possible.

We applied this. And it then appeared that the new energy source had more chance of succeeding if you prospect in areas in which you already produce, areas that represent sharp pencils - where we have a firm handle on the models. In contrast, if you explore in a totally new area, you have to set up everything without knowing whether the project is going to be profitable. To keep within the pencil metaphor, you have to sharpen that pencil from the start, but without knowing if you'll ever manage to get a sharp point on it.

The selected areas, on the other hand, the pencil is already sharp (there is no perfection in underground oil & gas). And so, working together, we arrived at the Big Rules: What do we have to take into account to increase our chances of success? In so doing, we had actually created a predictive model for future projects, with all the positive implications of such a tool, such as significant savings in terms of efficiency and an increase in effectiveness and success rate", says Sven.

He follows this fascinating account with how they are now applying the approach in practice.

"We are therefore making increasingly critical evaluations of whether a project matches the Big Rules. If the answer is 'yes', we have a big chance of continuing the process. If not, then we must be disciplined enough to stop applying it, before it goes wrong.

I do operate at mega high level. One shows a number of slides and makes a proposal and then the people in the country take that and get to work. And once I see that happening I step out of it. But in the case of the strategy for the new energy source I hung around, because I found what happened there very special", says Sven.

"It's so great when you see a result. They were using the sharpened approach, which was something in itself, and there was a positive result for our business, for our employees and for the surrounding area.

What I could recommend to everyone is focus on your current source of business. Look at the facts: Do not just go out and start the adventure anywhere and then go for it, full on. Things could go very wrong. The chance of things going wrong is much larger if you're in areas that are new to you, than in those where you already know all the ins and outs. The risk of something going wrong in unfamiliar territory is many, many times bigger - and that is the risk we have now reduced, with this new approach."

"You've been with Shell for a long time?" I ask.

"Yes", says Sven - in the manner of one contemplating this for the first time.

"In fact, for my whole working life. The funny thing is that when I had interviews at Shell there were people who'd worked for the company for ten, twelve, fifteen years - and I was amazed that they could have been with the same company for so long. I didn't understand it. Now I can identify with them completely - the international opportunities, job rotation, leadership development and travel are all things I've now also experienced and, indeed, have enjoyed very much. So I would now give the same answers if young people asked me why I've worked for this company for so long. I have had many different jobs. I have worked in different countries. I work for one of the largest and oldest companies in the world. In fact a company like this is a world in itself. It has everything. Yes, it has everything and, as a result, evolves and continues to re-invent itself as time passes. Which fascinates me no end.

Somewhere in our company smart men and women are busy right now, just like you, discovering their own Bitsing method and, in the process, applying it. Using it to develop smart things and trigger better and different ways of doing things. They also help drive the entire company, by continuously improving themselves. It's what we at Shell do, we're always improving ourselves. These people are spread throughout Shell, they are to be found in every department and country. And that is very inspiring."

"Looking at the Bitsing method as a strategist, at Shell, I think it has wide applications", says Sven. "I was also recently thinking about its application in searching for a job or career, and in the achievement of many other kinds of goals. This methodology automatically makes you think about the choices you are offered. You ask, 'Does this job offer fit the overall picture?' Instead of just taking any job. The whole career process could be approached more thoroughly and systematically. I haven't developed this any further yet. But there, too, lie many opportunities. There are so many applications. I think it's a great opportunity to investigate all these other applications and apply them."

Nothing would please me more than to tackle these tasks, together with Sven. Instead, I ask my last question: "You responded to my blog with, 'Bitsing remains impressive in its simplicity and accuracy'. It's great to hear this from someone who works for a company the size of Shell, in a complex area, and who has so much influence in the world."

Sven: "What we're after isn't something that's available off the shelf. Gigantic sums of money are involved and a lot of uncertainty.

And one has a lot of responsibility then, to the world. Because no one knows exactly what is under the ground. There are huge uncertainties, with many different aspects, in which a lot of money is involved. And a lot of responsibility - for instance to your employees and to the environment, to take just two aspects.

I would like to pass on the following advice: Keep making forecasts - and use that information to populate a financial model and a planning model. Try to keep this as fact-based as possible. For us at Shell, this is not an easy process. We don't know what is under the ground, or in a reservoir. And, to re-visit my example of the new energy source: whereas we originally invested in areas just because we thought we could be successful there (with investments that quickly rise to tens of billions), our forecasts are now significantly more fact-based, also using a Bitsing-like method.

So what I am basically saying is, don't just start up a project. At least make sure that you estimate the risks you're going to take, based on the facts to hand and taking all possible risk factors into account."

INTERVIEW 2 HEWLETT PACKARD ENTERPRISE

"IF YOU DO WHAT YOU'VE ALWAYS DONE, YOU GET WHAT YOU ALWAYS GOT."

MARTIJN BOERMANS

Bitsing is mainly based on information, data. Populating the models with data produces answers, which tell you what to do to achieve your goal. But what is data, actually? We've all heard of 'big data' ... that organisations are sitting on extremely large amounts of data. But what happens when that amount is **really** big? When it's from several sources. When there is so much of it that you no longer know what to do with it, or how to apply it?

Massive data volume
Let's visit one of the world's largest IT companies, Hewlett Packard Enterprise (HPE). They own the largest volume of large-business client data in the world.

How does HPE handle this amount of data? How do they select the right data from this mountain of information and apply it in such a way that the company grows?

I call on Martijn Boermans, Sales Program Manager EMEA (Europe, Middle East & Africa). Martijn initiates date-driven sales programmes and is responsible for their international rollout.

He's also a big Bitsing fan, so I start our conversation with this question:
"HPE is not only the largest IT company in the world, it also has an immense amount of data tucked away in various corners of the organisation. How do you structure this data - and then effectively and efficiently make it work for your organisation?"

Martijn: "It's not a simple task to work out what's useful, what you need for each task,

how to make choices, set priorities and know the extent to which you have to focus on them. These are the common problems with data. As are the issues of how to calculate your potential turnover and work out which resources will be most effective in extracting the maximum benefit. The Bitsing method and its models have helped me enormously in this. I'll try explain how I've applied it in my work with our international team."

Fully integrated Bitsing model
Martijn continues: "I started using Bitsing after reading your book. It was given to me by a business contact. This triggered me to deepen my understanding and take a master's course at Nyenrode University. There I was exposed to the background of the Bitsing method and got hands-on experience in applying the method to current HPE data. Which was very inspiring.

Significant start - significant insights
"It was clear from the start that the model and the methodology of information management yielded so many data points that I could make good use of the Bitsing scientific method. I extracted and converted the data relevant for Bitsing from our big data. I formed this into a single, integrated overview covering regions, countries, markets, customers, product lifecycles,

related sales activities and so on. Three substantial insights emerged from this:

Focus and clear prioritisation

We could immediately see which programmes were necessary for the coming year, as well as the relevant priorities and planning requirements. This focus clarified things enormously. The big data analyses and HPE information flows, in conjunction with our self-developed Bitsing overview, now direct our selection of the right product/market combinations. At the same time we get a visualisation of our strategic focus, our tactical product and operational marketing programs and, most importantly, the continuous turnover stream produced by these programmes.

Results, conversion ratios and the relative importance of our regions

What I really like is the insight we get into the development of the conversion rates, per Bitser step, as we roll out the various components of our sales programme (marketing, sales enablement, sales cycle management and after sales programs). We also get a great view of results by region and country. We can see conversion from prospect to lead and from lead to opportunity (the B, I and T scores).

And we can see the scores of the various sales stages within the pipeline and the conversion from pipeline to actual opportunities gained (S, E and R scores). The conversion ratios that emerge appear to be correct and are also in line with my results predictions.

Action to be taken

And finally, the third benefit of the model is, of course, a very clear view of what we have to do, at each of the six Bitser steps. As a result, the alignment of marketing processes at HPE has considerably improved.

As a result I've been able to link our targeted results to a continuous process of activity programme development. The programmes ensure continuity while maximising results."

Measurement!

I was impressed. "**So you've really derived your own model**", I said to Martijn. "Yes", he said. "It's still your, specific method - but basically I have developed systems that make it workable at HPE. The KPIs appear in my dashboard, with recaps showing actual results. You can immediately see where you're behind, where you're ahead and if your organisational focus is still correct. In fact, you can immediately

see the results of your efforts, your current situation and what you have to do next. Our self-developed dashboard literally shows red, amber or green lights. This happens automatically, via a live link with our sales information system, which gives access to the sales activities in our programmes and to current results. This also makes the dashboard interesting for our management. The information streams show, for instance, whether a country or region underperformed on certain programmes. Which we means we can offer help there." He laughs, "The benefit of Bitsing, huh!"

Martijn continues: "Regardless of what you take into account in your management process, when it comes to managing your programs the system tells you when your numbers need adjusting. So you see where the gaps are. Take the Bitser steps, for instance. There must be enough people on each step to sufficiently populate the next step, in order to achieve your goal. My Bitsing dashboard shows the types of red flag situations that develop. For example, if you have simply implemented too few promotions in the lower part of the BITSER ladder, the consequence will be that too few target group people end up in my BITSER pipeline. So if you have set your targets and want to achieve them, on a guaranteed basis, you have to (just as you indicated in the master's course) simply add more people at the bottom of the Bitser ladder. The gap analysis shows the gap that has developed over time. And it's perfectly visible and measurable, as a result of applying your method. One knows exactly how many people you need to add to a particular BITSER step and so you just develop BITSER programmes that do that job, using the sharpest pencils you have. You know what you have to do. You also know that if you don't do it, you won't achieve your goal. Filling these gaps becomes almost an automatic process."

"What is the most special experience you've had in applying the Bitsing method? Could you share that with us?"
Martijn: "It's the inspiration - especially from the master's program - and then the experience of applying that. I did an MBA. What one sees there is that people develop a different attitude as a result of the theory they have learned. This inspires them to build something new, also based on method. Which, in fact, was my experience with the Bitsing method. One also shouldn't accept everything unthinkingly. If everyone did that you'd all end up doing the same thing! I started by using your Bitsing method and then thought

up my own applications for it, which was tremendous. If all this hard work then leads to the discovery that it works - well, that's the ultimate!"

"What has it been worth to you, specifically?"
Martijn: "There are, of course, more factors involved than just the Bitsing method - as regards achievement of our goal. But in the year that followed my implementation of the BITSING programme, turnover increased by 168 percent! So we're not talking about a change worth thousands of euros - we're talking about millions. I believe that everyone here is very happy with this and I've also had a lot of international attention as a result. Which, of course, helps when it comes to the implementation of new programmes. These successes have a long-lasting effect."

"So what would you like to pass on to our readers?"
Martijn answers: "In relation to the Bitsing method - adopt it! Absorb the information, adopt the methodology - and find data points in the organisation that will support it. Analyse the information - bring your own perspective to it. Feel free and have fun! This is how you make it applicable to your situation. You can even use BITSING to

prove your own ideas and concepts. I adopted BITSING because I wanted to change something. My aim was to improve our programme by applying the method - and that worked exceedingly well. I'm always trying to make everything I do smarter and more efficient.

Our organisation has room for new ideas of this type, though you always have to prove their validity. So we still make relatively extensive use of MS Excel as an analysis tool. Now I'm looking for newer BI software - to further improve our insights into the data. Data engineering and data modelling (Big Data tooling) are undergoing huge development at the moment and I think we are ready for the next step in this regard. Because, if you just do what you've always done, you only get what you always got!"

INTERVIEW 3 SAINT-GOBAIN WEBER BEAMIX

> " YOU HAVE TO KEEP MOVING, ALWAYS. STANDING STILL MEANS YOU'RE GOING BACKWARDS."

BAS HUYSMANS

Saint-Gobain employs 190,000 people in 64 countries. The business has four divisions, each with its own area of expertise. These complement each other in such a way as to make this a global top 100 industrial company, in terms of both innovation and size. The business has seven general and twelve specialised, research institutes - and around a hundred development departments. These resources are used by each of the company's four divisions - innovative materials, building distribution, packaging materials and building products.

My interview is with Bas Huysmans, Managing Director of Saint-Gobain Weber Beamix, pioneers in the DIY market.

It focuses on the building product division.

How did you use the Bitsing method and what can you tell us about growing at a multiple of the market growth rate?
Bas Huysmans: "You have to keep moving, always. Standing still means you're going backwards. Or, to coin a saying, for us still waters don't run deep - they're just stagnant. To keep moving forward you sometimes have to let go of the security of the old way of doing things. Not easy for some people. In fact, for many in our business, using the Bitsing method was a journey into unknown territory. So people are of course a bit hesitant in the beginning, wondering what's going to happen. You always have to take this into account - so it pays to be patient and take things step by step. You don't have to get it 100% right the first time. People will take you seriously in due course.

What one discovers in this process is that many still use the 'I think that ...' approach. And indeed, people are used to working on the basis of assumptions. What we've now done is make things far more fact based - how things are, rather than how we think they are.

There was previously a mentality of, 'OK, I have a task, so it's up to me to do it - the way I think best'. People understood the Bitsing method well enough; the challenge was to get them to work according to it. So we integrated it into our daily operations, step by step. We started by creating awareness of the turnover goal and that everything we did should result in turnover. This was quite ambitious. Five years of recession had resulted in a damaged, unstable construction market. A closer look revealed that people were a bit numbed by the negative experiences of recent years. So we immediately started shifting the focus of the organisation - using the pencils philosophy of the Bitsing method. It emerged that we had invested a lot of time and money in markets, target groups, and products with less than significant shares in our turnover. It was inconceivable, but the vast majority of our turnover derived from 1.3% of our product range.

Shifting to a realistic focus resulted directly in 20% growth. The 'pencils' are a fantastic tool for convincing everyone in the organisation of the need to change focus.

This corrected focus led directly to active engagement with the market. We did this using an uncopyable proposition - our leading position as the pioneer of the DIY market: 'Lead by Origin'. Each of the involved departments took control of their own segment of the BITSER programme. B and I fell to marketing, T and S to sales and E and R to account management. They all developed their own programmes, with the common departure point being the essence of our Golden Egg: 'Lead by Origin'. Everyone in the organisation knew what this proposition meant. So the departments could independently, yet consistently, develop their own BI, TS and ER programmes. In conclusion, we assembled these elements into a consistent, BITSER programme, compiled by all of our departments. It was extraordinary to see how the awareness thus created integrated these previously independently operating departments. Now Marketing is aware that Sales can't sell without B and I, and Sales knows it must achieve the T and S in order that Account Management can retain the clients recruited by Sales,

failing which all the efforts of Marketing and Sales are wasted. A feeling of togetherness and collegiality emerged as a key element in our organisation.

First impressions were often negative - and old habits die hard. Initial reactions to new things were often, 'I'm already so busy', or 'Yes, but my approach is very different'. However, as the system ('What pencil are you using for that?') and the role of the departments within the BITSER model were better understood, acceptance became easier and is now almost automatic."

Can you describe what Bitsing has done for you - in one word?
"'Streamlined! That's the key word. You came here telling us that everyone within an organisation is busy doing their own thing, while not one of them is involved, from beginning to end, in the entire process. And yes, at Saint-Gobain Weber Beamix we had a Strategic department, Marketing department, a Sales department, an R&D department and a Production department - all doing their own thing. Of course they engaged each other and had points of contact, but nothing about the interplay was streamlined. So they weren't really working with and for each other. Indeed, it was this word, 'streamlined', that actually

triggered my reaction, which was, 'This is music to my ears!' We can do something with this, I thought. The structured approach inherent in Bitsing forces an organisation to also adopt a harmonised, structured approach in order to achieve its common aim. Which is why I then adopted the Bitsing system - a decision that has validated itself in practice.

The language of Sales is totally different to that of Marketing. Both departments endure a lot of pressure, do a lot of activities and suffer a lot of stress. However, they experience different types of pressure, action and stress, and express this in two, different languages. So it is difficult to have enough **empathy** with each other, given this barrier. It's difficult to engage with each other's opportunities and problems.

As a result of the Bitsing process, the organisation now shares a common language to a much greater extent. Everyone now knows how to identify an important product; that you can only get a client to buy once he likes you, and so on. It actually doesn't matter anymore whether you're on the marketing or sales side, or in production and innovation, you all speak the same language, you understand what is meant and you also see the effects of the work of others on your own part of the business. The inter-actions between the various disciplines are suddenly far more linked to each other and have become almost visual for the people in the various departments, particularly in Sales, Marketing and After Sales."

Does this give them more respect for each other's work?
Bas affirms, "Yes. Because you have better, shared understanding of what the other person is doing, and why you are doing these things. There is also more readiness on all sides to work with each other and help each other. So what we deliver is now seen as the product of everyone's efforts, which also has a motivating effect. This, in turn, creates more commitment and better performance - and so you have almost a virtuous cycle."

And what you're now doing is raising this to the next level?
"Yes, It's like learning a new language. In the first phase you really do your best to learn the words, the conjugations. So you get to know the language, but you don't yet speak it. As a company we are in that phase. We can get by with the language - perhaps on holiday, but when it comes to conducting business we are not yet fluent enough. Which is why I took the decision to become more fluent in the language."

What other effects have you noticed?
"Internally, I can see we're beginning to get more insight into the short term - our plans are better. Where we once operated on gut feel in terms of product development and promotions, we are now more planning orientated and therefore can also prepare our internal operations better. So, as regards development - we are more focused on developing. And in Marketing and Sales we are more targeted in our approach. We've experienced distinct advantages in both these areas. Now that Marketing and Sales give more consideration to what we have to do, it's become noticeably easier to communicate their expectations to Production and Logistics.

What's really difficult is not doing the things that we've always done. People have a tendency, in the first instance, to do Bitsing in addition to what they used to do. They see it as increased workload - 'Now they've thought up another one'. But as they take the first steps and start to make progress, they become more enthusiastic and more aware of the fact that Bitsing actually reduces workload."

Are you growing at the moment?
Bas: "Yes. Our growth rate is at least twice that of the market. Which means that we are grabbing market share. And, of course, there's a reason for that. It's partly due to the organisation itself, with its well-struc-tured management. And that, in turn, is a function of the fact that we are more highly focused. And that the decisions we have taken are far more based on facts than feelings. We do still follow our gut feelings, but the decision process has been speeded up enormously by the fact that we've looked at the Bitsing plan. And this, in turn, has given us a far better understanding of the numbers. When you first arrived, Frans, we had just survived a five-year crisis. Things were just lightening up again. We were able to breathe again. You came with a positive message, a very simple message. One that I, as a technical guy, could easily understand. That was very important. It's as simple as it can be. And you presented it in such a simple way that everyone that heard it said, 'Yes, of course, we knew that all along - so yes, let's do it!' It's so logical, it must work. Yes, you arrived at the right moment, with the right message. One that appealed to my need to shake up the internal organisa-tion, organise it better and tighten up the processes. Your logic appealed to me - as did the simplicity of the system. It's what persuaded me to adopt Bitsing!

Every entrepreneur wants results. There is no shortage of people who invest millions in projects while having no idea of what the investment will produce - as strange as this seems. The success of Bitsing stands or falls in relation to how strictly one executes the Bitsing plan. If we were to partially apply it, it wouldn't work. Of course you can do other things alongside it - one has to retain a bit of individuality - but I really am convinced that half doing it makes absolutely no sense.

With Bitsing it's not a question of a promotion here and a campaign there. You have to do the whole thing. That's what resulted in our growth. If we hadn't Bitsed, we may have done these activities in any event, but would then perhaps only have had 25% of the total, required package in place. And what would that have delivered, if anything? By thinking it through completely, from a to z, one develops the complete process. As a result, your prospects and clients swim further into the net, making it more difficult for them to escape. Yes, we did previously conduct similar activities. We put the nets into the water, but we hung the bait near the entrance. Clever fish entered, then quickly turned around and swam in the opposite direction. Now we have six pieces of Bitser bait and the fish swim so far into the net that they can't escape.

And because they are always addressed in a way that's appropriate to the Bitser step they are on, the fish are always happy!

The system is complete. The 'Lead by Origin' message is everywhere. On our fleet, our videos, in our promotions and TV commercials, our online presence and so on. We have delivered so many solutions in so many areas that we have built up really extensive experience over the last 50 years. In principle, we've already executed a solution for virtually every problem that arises - and it's in our records. We can do anything that's required. Which is why the whole Saint-Gobain Weber Beamix enterprise is designed around flexibility - it's an important pillar of the organisation. So everything that we do and everything that we invest in must increase our flexibility - and certainly never limit it.

What I would like to pass on to the reader is that you shouldn't limit yourself to a few products or single target group. This exposes your business to risk. If the market collapses, you're done for. In Bitsing 'pencil' terminology, deriving your turnover from only one pencil product or target group makes you very vulnerable, especially if you can't sharpen the pencil. Broaden your range and use the pencils philosophy to achieve this.

There will always be ups and downs, but a good mix ensures that you can operate comfortably in your market. Bitsing helped us to focus and concentrate - and sometimes to drop a few things. Things which didn't generate turnover, or weren't profitable. We did that, and we didn't go unrewarded. We are currently growing at a rate of 22%."

INTERVIEW 4 SELECTA

"DREAM IT. BELIEVE IT. ACHIEVE IT."

KRISTIEN JANSEN

As I enter Selecta's offices the first thing that greets me is the authentic and delicious aroma of fresh coffee. Selecta is the leading vending and coffee services company in Europe. The market leader (with a turnover of more than 740 million euros) employs 4,300 motivated people, who provide 6 million customers in 18 countries with self-selected coffee, soda, snacks and candy on a daily basis, from 140,000 workplace and public sales points. The company was founded in 1957 in Switzerland, where its head office is located.

I'm visiting commercial director Kristien Jansen. Before starting the interview I help myself to a delicious cup of coffee, sit down and enjoy what Kristien has to say how about setting goals, the creation of a positive brand experience, cooperation with top brands like Starbucks and the achievement of success. (Kristien was elected Commercial Director of the Year!)

"Participating in such an election is great fun. But winning the award is obviously a nice boost. At the same time the next day is just business as usual, with or without this prestigious award". That's Kristien all over, sensible and down to earth. "You don't want to get carried away by these things", she says. "Two other women also made it to the final round. That was very unusual, because it is such a male preserve.

So if three women make it to the podium it's great. They weren't there because they were women. They were there as a result of their performance and, of course, to win the prize. The fact that I won it does not, of course, diminish their individual achievements."

Nevertheless, the jury thought you had earned the award. Would you like to share what you did with our readers?
"To achieve your ambitions, it is necessary that you have a clear goal. For me that goal is always linked to turnover growth. Because: no profit without turnover. That's what appealed to me so much about the Bitsing method - that you use turnover as your goal and focus all the resources of the organisation in the achievement of that turnover goal. Financial resources are, of course, necessary for growth. When I joined Selecta we had little financial resources to invest. If that's a fact, you'll just have to deal creatively with that situation – which is what I did. It appears that I had quite a few opportunities that I could deploy to achieve growth.

My ambition is to be number one in terms of the coffee experience. I put this question to my colleagues when I first came to work here and I got many different answers.

So we first asked ourselves on how we want our customers to experience us. And ultimately, Frans, you used your Bitsing method to help us find our Golden Egg, which defined our point of difference. Or, to use Bitsing terminology, made us uncopyable. The outcome was so simple, but so true. It was something that had always lain hidden in our organisation, but which we had never raised."

That was your independence wasn't it? Being independent is what makes Selecta uncopyable?
Kristine answers, "Yes! Selecta has three USPs. The first is that we are European market leader. This means that we have an organisation with room for innovation; one in which we are supported by plenty of expertise and a wealth of best practices. This enables us to behave and operate like a market leader, even in countries in which we are not. Our second USP is that we offer the best service. This is widely acknowledged and is supported by the fact that Starbucks chose us, as it's exclusive partner. And if Starbucks selects you...well, everyone knows how proud Starbucks is of their brand and that they wouldn't share it with just anyone. Which is where our third USP becomes relevant - the Golden Egg. We can always offer the solutions that fit our clients,

because we are independent, not tied to a particular brand of coffee, nor coffee machine. Bitsing helped us enormously in identifying our Golden Egg and also in identifying other USPs. The score map analysis showed us where we really differentiate ourselves from competition".

So how did you use that; what did you do with it?
Kristien: "We expressed our independence in the theme of **unlimited enjoyment.** With Selecta, enjoyment is unlimited - and we used this uncopyable theme to communicate with our environment. With our employees, our clients, our prospects and with other stakeholders. The Golden Egg supports the sales department in so far as it enables it to easily express what differentiates us. Look, what I believe is that when you're selling something, which really contributes to the achievement of your client's goals, you will make the difference. Our clients are all unique. They all have different objectives. So for us the task is very much focused on how we can ensure that each solution fits the client's needs.

Does your independence enable you to deliver that? Does it make you indeed uncopyable in relation to other market players?

Kristien: "Yes! That's the important thing - the Golden Egg. That's what Bitsing has made clear to us. Another important thing: it made us think about our resources and the selection of media in the marketing, sales and after sales process.

It starts with the B. This is where we commence our carefully structured approach to our prospects. Our target group is facility managers. You have to stand out in order to gain awareness in this target group. We achieved this by sending them cookie tins bearing our name. We developed this campaign two years ago and are still using it."

At the time you did a test on a very small number of recipients. Only when this proved successful did you approach the entire market.
Kristien: "That's right. We dispatch cookie tins every month, pro rata to the number of 'I's we require and the number of visits ('T's) we need in the relevant period. This makes it much easier for the marketing and sales departments to follow up with the next step and we get a significant improvement in conversion from B to I and I to T."

So how did you do the I and the T?
"Well, the cookie tin arrives empty. But when you open it you confront the first step towards the I: a flyer in the tin refers you to a teaser website, where you can order your own cookies. You, the customer, determine what happens, you make independent (our Golden Egg) decisions, you order your own cookies - and then we deliver. And so this is the first promotion towards the T. When we deliver the cookies you've ordered we make a follow-up appointment, for the real, hard T meeting. We use a tailor-made, risk-free non-commercial traffic offer for this. When we did the test it was an offer of sharing research information of an independent (coffee) survey amongst thousand employees.

Our current, risk-free offer depends on the topic, on what is happening at that time. So at one time it could be 'the Coffee survey', at another 'fair trade', or 'sustainability'. It's always a general subject, but one that always relates to the experience of coffee and our independency. Now, for instance, we're sending cookie tins to a selection of the businesses that rank in 'Great place to work'.

The interesting thing is that we thought this up ourselves. External agencies are often used for that, but we didn't have the budget.

We were facing a growth challenge but we also had to make profit. So we had to be creative with the resources that we had. In this situation you have to consider your options carefully. You can only spend the money once, so the question is, what do you invest it in?"

So you put a whole lot of effort into getting this right, but what did it ultimately deliver? Did it have effect and if so what?
"We had experienced a three-year decline, but after one year of Bitsing we had broken this trend and accomplished turnover growth. My team did this by no longer investing in blunt pencils: markets, target groups, products and initiatives. Instead we used the available time in a productive way, as prescribed by the pencils analysis. In addition, we compared our marketing, sales and after sales activities with the Bitser steps, to check that each target group on a particular step was getting the attention it deserved. This provided a clear overview of the roles of our marketing and sales departments, as well as account management. While previously marketing had expected sales to do everything and, of course, vice versa. We got a lot of help in making the right choices by checking, a few times a year, where we are investing our time and available budget - using the pencils analysis and the BITSER steps."

So what role will Bitsing play in your future?
Kristien is firm. "We will keep using it. It's automatic now - part of our daily processes. It defines what we have to do. For instance if our European market leader position means we have to innovate, if we have to try out something new, we no longer blindly commit people and use budgets already allocated for other purposes. We don't touch them. We examine step by step whether the innovation will develop into something worthwhile, whether it has the potential to become a sharp pencil. We also do things like entering partnerships in order to limit risks and maintain the correct degree of focus. When you are forced to not just throw money at an opportunity you become far more creative in your approach."

And then you received the commercial director of the year award.
Kristien continues, her tone modest, "Yes, I am proud that we turned the trend around in the two and a half years that I've been here. My motto is 'dream it, believe it, achieve it'. Which is also about our dream - to be the number one coffee experience. You have to make your dream concrete. Each department has given its own interpretation to our dream. Keeping our core values and Golden Egg in mind.

Then it's a question of believing in your dream! At our company this was quite difficult to achieve because how do you make a difference in a market that is characterized as a commodity. We quickly found evidence. I commissioned research among thousand employees. What emerged was that coffee does make the difference. More than 59% of employees get a boost from a good cup of coffee. So we had something to work with. We could make a contribution and make the difference with our Golden Egg. Also: if Starbucks believed in us, we should believe in ourselves. If someone else likes you it's logical that you should like yourself. Our dream is therefore legitimate, because it's realisable.

So then you must get to work and achieve it. But how do you do that?
There were issues. For instance, we just weren't getting appointments with our prospects, which was frustrating. Then we started working with you - and Bitsing. We started applying the six BITSER steps and using the simple cookie tin device. In the first tranche we already achieved a nearly 20% conversion. Which was, of course, fantastic! We also had to work on our relationship management. A major prospect, a financial institution, told us that they wanted to issue a tender in a year's time.

In the meeting with them I realised that we just weren't in a situation in which we could be the ones that made the difference. We appeared as just another supplier. So, with all our employees from operations, marketing, sales and account management, we literally went and stood next to their coffee machines - in order to ask their employees what could be different and better. Our independence (Golden Egg) enabled us to try out a number of concepts in order to find out which best suited the requirements of their employees. And this resulted in a five-year contract. By getting our employees to look at the situation, literally through the eyes of the client, we delivered a tailor-made solution and are able to really apply our point of difference: unlimited enjoyment, through our independence.

All of this is actually about just doing things. You have to just do it! And you have to take the organisation with you in this. Literally. You have to feel it! Be inspired by 'dream it, believe it, achieve it'. It's my motto - both in business and private life. When I presented the growth plan to our team the dream was visible on the first slide. It was our turnover goal and it represented an ambitious increase. The second slide stated that 'we must believe that we can do this'. The final slide set out what we had

to do to achieve the goal. We review our previous year's performance annually. I conducted an evaluation with our entire team. Then I showed them those slides again - and was able to say, 'See...it's happened, we achieved it'.

We achieved our turnover growth and turned around a negative growth trend. We increased our client satisfaction or Net Promoter Score (NPS)* from negative to positive, by a multiple of 6.5. A negative score tells you that customers advise others to avoid you. Now the vast majority undertake referral business for us. There has been a massive increase in loyalty. Our employees are significantly more satisfied. Our annual motivational research shows that the organisation is both more inspired and more involved.

So we achieved three successes: we've reversed the negative growth trend, we've improved client satisfaction and our employees are happier. And that's how you become commercial director of the year!" Kristien smiles broadly - and with some justification. It's an award well earned.

* Client satisfaction methodology developed in 2003 by Satmetrix, Bain & Company and Fred Reichheld.

A WISH

Please return to bitsing.com/growth and answer a brief question. Something unexpected has happened to you. Do it today, because you have a lot of 'bitsness' coming up. Whether you apply the Bitsing method on your own or with hundreds, or thousands, of co-workers, do so in the knowledge that nobody has to change and that this is not an additional burden, but actually a process that lightens the load. It's not change, in itself, but will lead to positive changes in motivation and results. As I often say, 'Bitsing does not ask you to change, it is just a different way of dealing with existing information'.

I WILL LEAVE YOU WITH A WISH... THAT YOU WILL ACHIEVE ALL THE RESULTS THAT YOU STRIVE FOR AND ENJOY THEM TO THE FULL THIS IS WHY YOU ARE ON EARTH, TO FULLY ENJOY THE POSITIVE THINGS IN LIFE. SINCE DISCOVERING THE BITSING METHOD, I HAVE COME TO REALISE THAT ANYTHING IS POSSIBLE. I HOPE TO HAVE INSTILLED THIS BELIEF IN YOU. IF SO, I HAVE ACHIEVED MY GOAL

And finally: Base your decisions and actions as far as possible on facts. Be assured, everything you do will succeed. The wish is not father to the thought - facts are!

Till we meet again,

Frans de Groot

FORSEEING
IS....

THE ESSENCE OF GOVERNANCE

THANK YOU

When I finally got to setting down the first words of this book I had to think of the people who, consciously and subconsciously, were also involved in laying the foundations of the Bitsing method. Without them I would never have come so far with the development of the Bitsing method or with this book.

In particular I want to thank John Holloway who, with his historic statement:

> " FRANS, YOU'RE ON THE BUS OR OFF THE BUS."

This statement made me jump on the bus.

I decided to quit my job to start a marketing communication agency with him, where I laid the foundation of the Bitsing method. Then there was, of course, Arjen de Jong, former MD of the BMW, Land Rover,

MG and Mini automotive group, who had the courage to implement the plan from which the basic BITSER model emerged, thus enabling me to discover the method and its effects.

Thanks also to Prof. Dr. Jac Vennix, Chair of Research Methodology Radboud University, The Netherlands and (Former) Executive Director of the European Master Programme in System Dynamics (EMSD). He revealed the method's real, scientific basis. Further thanks are due to him for providing this book with a foreword - of which I'm really proud. Not to be forgotten are the Bitsing coaches. They provide support for the coaching of organisations - and thus helped me findthe time to write this book.

Thanks also to Rudolf van Wezel and Bionda Dias of BIS Publishers, the publisher of this book. Their belief in the international publication of the book on Bitsing methodology brings the opportunity to successfully apply Bitsing to a worldwide audience. Thank you!

Last but not least, I very special thank you to Annette Oudejans - who initiated and produced the book - and my family for their support in times of writer's block and especially for motivating me to leave my little footprint in eternity with this book.

Frans de Groot